CARING FOR "BAMBI"

REHABILITATING WHITE-TAILED DEER FAWNS

BY

DANA SIMS

Table of Contents

FROM THE AUTHOR

IN LOVING MEMORY OF MY MOTHER AND "BESTEST" GAL

NANCY

How this book came to be

I don't know about you, but whenever I read a rehabilitation book or article, I want to know what kind of experience the author has.   I'm more apt to listen to someone who's been doing this for decades than someone with just a few years experience.   I tend to heed someone's advice who has worked with hundreds of a species over someone who's handled just a few.   I give more credence to a rehabber's suggestions if she has a good, solid reputation over one whose feedback is less than impressive (however, I never make a judgment based on gossip).   Because I would want to know if the person behind the information is reliable, I am including my qualifications...I figure you are going to wonder, too.

I have been a state and federally licensed rehabilitator in North Carolina since 1991.   During that time, I have learned a lot about...and cared for... nearly every indigenous species in my state (and very large numbers of them as well).   Yet there aren't many species I would write a book about.   Frankly, I wouldn't have written this one except for repeated and fervid requests from rehabbers familiar with my deer background wanting a detailed, yet easy to understand, guide on caring for fawns.

In addition to rehabilitating fawns and helping the public with injured deer situations for nearly 18 years, I oversaw our state's fawn program for 12.   I've had hands-on experience with well over a thousand fawns at the state facility, plus hundreds at my own.

The state ran a fawn rehabilitation program for decades before I came onto the scene.   It is that program I started out under as a fawn rehabber.   There were nine of us and we each covered a significant sized area of the state.   It was our responsibility to care for and stabilize fawns until they were transferred to the primary facility.   A special permit (over and above our state rehabilitator's license) was required and only one per district (9) were issued.   Being a deer rehabber was a big deal and a great honor.

When I became the fawn rehab coordinator, I initiated changes to make the fawns healthier and happier at the state facility.   I then worked with the other fawn rehabbers to establish some consistency among us, such as requiring use of the same formula and nipples as the state was using.   Transfer of the fawns from rehabber to state facility was traumatic enough without an immediate change of diet and feeding instruments as well.   By the same token, I had no desire to interfere with each rehabber's individualism either, knowing I would not like it if someone did that to me.   I always made certain to look at issues from all sides of the coin – the state, the rehabbers, the public, but most importantly, the fawns.

Due to concerns over CWD, North Carolina shut down the fawn program on January 1, 2003.   It became illegal to rehab deer and the state's impressive facility was literally dismantled.   As you can imagine, it created a lot of controversy.   The regulation was overturned six months later and I was asked to create, implement, and oversee a new program, one that would no longer involve a state facility.   It was well into fawn rehab season, so it was crucial to move quickly because lives were literally at stake.   I went to work on it that very day.   It was a massive and overwhelming undertaking (especially for one person), yet I knew I could not handle the guilt if I said no.

The new program allowed for the end of hard releasing fawns - something I had wanted to see for a long time.   Rehabilitators would now be able to take in fawns, stabilize and care for them, then soft-release from the pen they were raised in.   A new program would allow for several other changes that I was pleased about.

The experience and information I had gained as fawn rehabber and coordinator gave me the foundation to create this new program.   I built upon the extensive experience of those who came before me, added changes I felt were warranted, took out what we had learned didn't work, and from there the new fawn program was born.   Considering the limited resources available, I thought everything was going very well.   We had a dedicated team of volunteers across the state.   What we lacked in numbers we more than made up for in devotion.

After three years of steady progress, things changed yet again.   (What's that old adage about nothing being certain except change?)   Unfortunately, this time the modifications were not ones I could support.   It was heartbreaking because I had given so much for so long to this cause.   It felt as if twelve years of hard work disappeared in the blink of an eye.

Shortly after leaving, top management at the Commission gave me a gorgeous plaque thanking me for my years of volunteer work on the fawn program.   Normally I'm not big on plaques, but this one is beautiful and means a lot.

Although I have a lot of deer experience, I don't know everything there is to know about fawns...and don't claim to.   The rehabilitator who thinks she knows it all (on any subject) is dangerous.   There is always more to learn.   In addition, my way is not the only way.

There are many right ways when it comes to fawn care...there are many wrong ways, as well. Getting sick, injured, or orphaned wildlife to live is only part of the equation.   We must also get them to where they can survive and thrive once released.   Otherwise, we have not done our jobs.

So though I do not claim this book contains the only way to raise fawns, it does contain tried and true methods.   These did not come out of a lab manual or from research notes of someone who has never been near a fawn.   These are "field tested" techniques that work.

Regardless of what species you have rehabbed in the past, fawns are very different.   Even rehabilitators with decades of experience caring for other species have said so.   I hope this book will help you get to know and care for these extraordinary creatures.   Be forewarned...they are addictive!

Happy rehabbing!

Words of thanks

Above all, I want to thank my husband, Peter, who has given up any semblance of a normal life to take this "wild" journey with me.   We have been married almost 29 years and counting.   We've had animals all those years, but it started with just one dog.   It sort of exploded from there.   My husband is the kindest, most patient, loving, caring human being I know (he was probably a dog in a former life...and that's a high compliment in case you weren't certain!)   He has given up so much for this work, yet he never complains.   He is a constant and tireless champion for animals, making tremendous sacrifices.   He is my hero. It may sound trite to say, but it is true.

It would be unfair not to thank Harlan Hall, supervising biologist, who was charged with overseeing my work. Though he and I seldom agree on anything, I learned a lot from him... and hopefully taught him a thing or two along the way, as well!   I know of no other person who angered, frustrated or upset me more than he, but he did teach me a lot about deer.

My thanks also go to those few special fawn rehabbers (you know who you are) who joined the program at the beginning, grew with it, and made me very proud.

I have worked long and hard on this book during times I did not want to.   My precious, beloved mother battled a rare cancer for a very long time, but the last year she fought harder and endured more pain and procedures than one could imagine.   Sadly her fight came to an end the day after Christmas, and our family lost the sun, moon, and stars.   My Mother and I are extremely close, always have been.   It was both my onus and my honor to be with her 24/7 the last ten days of her life.   The pain is still very raw.   Quite honestly, I wanted to toss this book into the woodstove and be done with it.   I did not have the heart to finish it. However, I knew I needed to complete what I started and deliver what I promised.   After all, my mother would expect no less.

How to use this book

Although the book is fairly self-explanatory, there are a few things to know before beginning.

I think it is <u>very</u> important to read the book from start to finish at least once.   After that, you can refer to various chapters or subjects as needed, but I think it would be inadvisable to start off that way.

For the most part, rather than repeat things, if one section has information that ties in with another, I note that and refer you back to it.   I include the page number to make it easy to find.

Since I hate reading books that constantly use he/she, him/her, his/hers, etc., I refer to rehabilitators as "she," veterinarians as "he," and deer as "he" (unless specifically discussing a doe).   I am a rehabilitator and female, so I used she.   The veterinarian kind enough to contribute to this book is a man, so I utilized he when referring to vets.   I'm a feminist if ever there was one so there are no hidden meanings or agenda!   I am well aware many rehabbers are male and lots of vets are female.

I am a rehabilitator, not a veterinarian.   Any advice involving medication comes from a licensed vet.   As for the natural healing approaches detailed, I have used herbs, supplements, and other natural methods for well over 20 years.   They've been used on me, my husband, family, pets, and wildlife with amazing results.   Just keep in mind, nothing is without risk.   Even ingesting water can prove dangerous if done improperly (too much quantity in too short a time period, for example).   There is a very wide margin of safety with herbs and supplements (which is one reason I like using them), but you should know what you are doing.   Natural healing not only works, but works on "biggies" too…not just hangnails and itchy skin, but congestive heart failure and internal bleeding.   I encourage you to learn all you can about nature's medicines.   I cannot imagine running my facility without them.

I used a larger than normal type for this book.   Not that I need larger type (yeah right) but when looking up information in a hurry, it's easier if the words are a good size.

This book is geared toward those new to fawn rehabilitation and written with that in mind. Though I know the medical terms (most of them anyway!), I chose not to use them.   A new rehabber will have plenty of time later to learn the vocabulary.   When I was starting out, rehabbers who used lots of medical jargon and big words only made me feel ignorant.   So in this book, any medical terms or big words will be in parentheses or as an "oh, by the way."   I talk to you the way I like to be talked to - like one friend helping another.   As such, I include a number of personal stories.   Those are noted and in a different type. Although geared toward new deer rehabbers, there is lots of information for those who have been doing this a while, as well.

I have tried to cover nearly every subject related to deer.   One topic this book will not cover, though, is law.   Not only do wildlife regulations differ by state, but in some what's officially on the books is not necessarily followed.   In addition, laws can change.   It is beyond the scope of this book to cover all that for each of the 50 states.   If you have questions regarding wildlife laws and deer, contact the agency that oversees wildlife and rehabilitation (such as Wildlife Resources Commission or Department of Natural Resources) in your area.

Although much of the information in this book can be applied to permanent captive situations, not all can.   Laws in your state governing captive deer will dictate how some things are done.

There are many types of deer.   This book is specifically for rehabilitating white-tailed deer. I imagine much is applicable to other types, but I do not know what is and what is not.   I have no experience with the other types of deer.

I have worked hard to make sure all information is accurate.   I've also spent an inordinate amount of time proofing, editing, re-editing, rewording, tweaking, and thinking of more things to add.   I finally realized if I waited until it was "perfect," it would never get done. I feel certain the moment it gets mailed out, I will think of more details to add, wish I had worded things differently, or find a typo or two.

I have tried to make this book as detailed as possible, but it would take thousands of pages to cover everything there is to know about rehabbing deer.   Still, I think this is one of the most comprehensive books available on the subject.   I'm kind of proud of it anyway.

Disclaimer: This book was written for one reason – to help those who want to help fawns.   I am giving you what I believe to be the best advice and information currently available based on my many years experience.   However, no two situations are the same and the author (i.e. me!) cannot be held responsible for how this information is used or the results from using the information in this book.

(*Author's note*: *When I first started working with the other fawn rehabbers setting up guidelines for what formula, nipples, etc. to use (so it would match what was being used at the state facility), one of the rehabilitators contacted me, extremely upset.   She had used kaolin pectin for a deer that came in with diarrhea.   She insisted she had never lost a deer with diarrhea, therefore it had to be the kaolin pectin.   I assured her it is a very safe product and was not the cause of her deer dying.   I told her she could give the deer an entire bottle (not that I was advising anyone do so) and it still not kill the deer.   The point, though, is she believed the product (and thus, I) was to blame for the deer's demise.   It made me realize how easily I could be blamed for any advice I shared…thus the disclaimer.)*

SUPPLIES & WHERE TO FIND THEM

One question I am often asked is - what supplies do I need for rehabbing fawns?   The answer varies because not everyone does things the same way.   Not all the items on my list are essential.   You might choose to use different supplies.   The list (below) does not include what you will need to build your pen because every person's enclosure will differ in design and size.

It is important that you read the book first to determine which supplies best suit your needs. I would not recommend ordering from this list without reading the book, especially the care information chapters.

Supplies can be purchased from any number of places, either locally or online.   However, a few sources are provided in case you do not have a local supplier or don't wish to spend time searching online.   I have personally dealt with the companies listed and have had good service.   (My recommending these companies in no way implies they endorse this book nor have they in any way contributed financially to my organization.)

Item numbers are listed to make things easier and are correct at the time of publication. However, numbers can change, so be sure the item matches the description before ordering. I have not listed actual prices since those, too, can change, but I am listing an approximate cost.

Many herbs and supplements are now sold in supermarkets, super stores, and drugstores. However, not all products are created equal.   If you purchase an inferior brand, you are throwing your money away because it will not work, at least not well, so buy high quality brands.   By the same token, herbs are relatively inexpensive.   I have found that any natural product that's "sky high," especially if it professes to cure everything from athlete's foot to cancer, is a product to avoid.

My recommended supply list

the basics

pliable baby bottles

non-pliable baby bottles

nipples

formula

goat chow

bucket, bowl or feeder for the grain

bedding

extra large dog crates

bowl or bucket for water

colostrum

Nutridrench

nice extras

sound machine

camera to document your cases

natural medicines - the most critical

probiotics

slippery elm bark (herb)

vitamin E oil

black tea bags

garlic oil

hawthorn berries (herb)

Rescue Remedy (tincture)

horsetail (herb)

cayenne (spice)

cornsilk (herb)

uva ursi (herb)

gingko biloba (herb)

vitamin C (supplement)

hydrangea (herb)

meadowsweet (herb)

lady's slipper (herb)

licorice root (herb)

lobelia (herb)

aloe vera gel

arnica (homeopathy)

non-prescription medicines

kaolin pectin

simethicone

bloat release

antihistamine

Jeffers - 1-800-JEFFERS

www.jefferspet.com

This is a mail-order supplier of items for pets, cattle, goats, pigs, sheep, horses, etc. You can access their website on-line or call for a catalog. Ask for one each: pet, cattle, and goat catalogs because some items are in one and not the other. Items marked with an * are those I have personally used. Those without an * are ones you might be interested in trying, but I have not used that particular item or brand.

Some items from Jeffers you may want to purchase are:

- Goat colostrum* - #KK-G5 - powder - 9 oz. jar w/scoop (app. $10)

- Goat Nutri-drench* - #B8-N9 - 1 pint (app. $17)

- Lambar feeding outfit - #CL-01- complete unit (app. $45)

- Fortiflex fence bucket* - #FX-F7 (colors) or FX-F8 (black) - hooks over chain link so deer don't tip over (app. $10)

- Diaque - #FH-D1- 3.5 ounces (app. $2.50)

- Bloat Release* - #A2-B4 - 12 ounces (app. $3.50)

- Kao-Pec* - #A2-K2 - 1 gallon (app. $6)

- Trap-n-Toss flytrap* - #FA-T5 (app. $4)

- Pritchard lambs nipples* - #M6-P1 (app. $2)

- Probios probiotics granules* - #PN-P7 (app. $20)

- Large dog crates* - #3R-M6, 3R-M7, 3R-M8 or DK-VC (app. $65- $80)

- I-D bands - #EZ-E4-26 – box of 50 (app. $8)

Vitamin Shoppe - 1-800-223-1216

www.vitaminshoppe.com

This is a vitamin and supplement mail-order store.   They sell primarily human products but many items can be used with non-human animals as well.   Items marked with an * are ones I have personally used.   Those without an * are ones you might be interested in, but I have not used that particular item or brand.

Some items from Vitamin Shoppe you may want to purchase are:

- garlic oil* - #NW-7041 - Nature's Way (app. $7)

- Ultimate 10 Probiotics* - #VS-2164 - powder/capsule (app. $15)

- colostrum capsules - #VS-1607 - capsules (app.$14)

- Ultimate Fiber* - #SD-1007 - Nature's Secret - powder (app. $15)

- slippery elm bark* - #NW-1210, NH1127, or SO1234 - capsules (app. $8) (note: it is important to use a capsule/powder, not a tincture or gel cap)

- vitamin E oil - #EC-1053 - Home Health (app. $5)

Most, if not all, the other herbs and supplements listed under Nature's Medicine Cabinet can be found here.

Penn Herb - 1-800-523-9971

www.pennherb.com

This company specializes in herbs, as well as proprietary herbal blends.   They sell not only capsules, but bags of herbs as small as one ounce.   If there's an herb you may only use a scant small amount of, there's no need to buy a whole bottle.   You can find herbs at Penn you can't find other places.   I have been dealing with them for decades.   Their capsules are twice the size of other companies, so bear that in mind when comparing prices and figuring doses.

Most, if not all, the herbs and supplements listed under Nature's Medicine Cabinet can be found here.

<u>Sources for shade cloth:</u>

Shade cloth can be purchased from local hardware stores, such as Lowe's or Home Depot. You can find it at most farm services stores.   I know at least one person who got hers on E-bay.   I suggest an online search to compare prices against local sources.   If purchasing online, don't forget to take into account the shipping charges.

RECORD INFORMATION

Each state has their own regulations regarding record keeping.   Even if not required, I think it is important to fill out a report form for each deer just to keep general information on each patient.   I know some rehabilitation centers keep daily track of an animal's weight, as well as every ounce they consume.   My personal view is it's unnecessary when only one caregiver is involved.   Weighing a fawn is difficult and stressful to both the deer and the provider.   I see no benefit to continued weighing.   I also don't keep track of exactly how much each fawn takes in.   For one thing, with their propensity for bottle switching, it is impossible to know which fawn consumed how much.   Do yourself a favor and not worry about it, except in certain situations where a fawn is sick and details are more crucial.

My initial notes on a fawn include gender; approximate age; what happened (attacked by a dog, orphaned, kidnapped, hit by car, etc.); how much time elapsed from the injury/event until the fawn made its way into my care; what had been done for the fawn during that time; what type of injuries or illness I'm dealing with; what medicines have been used and how much; what I am doing for him; and what the prognosis is.   My future notes are less detailed.   They might say - fawn stable, continuing same medications, fever down, eating well - or - stopped all medications, fawn growing, doing well. -   In most cases, that is all that is needed.   This is especially true when there is only one caregiver (which at our facility is the case with every patient).

AGING & SEXING FAWNS

Determining if a fawn is male or female is pretty easy.   To begin with, a little buck is born with two dark swirls of hair on his forehead where the antlers will later form.   Then there's the genitalia, of course.   On a male, the genitals are higher whereas a female's are right in front of the anus.   You can sometimes tell a male from a female just by watching them urinate.

If only telling age were so simple.   I am frequently asked how to determine the age of a fawn.   I sometimes josh and say - first, you count all the spots, then you divide by...and wait to see how long it takes the person to catch on that I'm teasing.   But the truth is, there is no good way to tell.   The best way to determine age is by doing this work for many years. After taking in a lot of newborns and seeing how they develop at week one, week two, and so on, you will eventually be able to estimate age just by appearance.

If a fawn comes in with a still-wet umbilical cord, you know he is very new.   Another sign a fawn has just been born is the hooves are covered in a soft, gelatinous substance to prevent the placental sac from being punctured.   It wears off the first day.   Hooves are a lighter color at birth and get darker in a few days, another way of telling a very young fawn.

The umbilical cord dries up around the third day and drops off before the fawn is two weeks old.   These are all factors in aging a newborn.   After that, though, there are not a lot of good indicators, except, as I indicated, those you learn from experience.

At birth, a fawn's eyes (the pupils) are typically brown with the surrounding area (the iris) a bluish color.   Around 10 days old, that blue begins to turn brown.   However, this is not a reliable way of judging age because there are just too many cases of fawns a few days old with brown eyes and many well over 10 days old with blue.

CAGING/HOUSING RECOMMENDATIONS

Indoor housing for small fawns

Very young fawns (less than two weeks old), or fawns that are very weak or sick, can be kept indoors in a large dog crate in a room/area used primarily for wildlife rehabilitation. These should be the hard plastic crates that are screwed together (top and bottom) and have a metal door that swings open. Most also have metal grate-style "windows" on the side. Be sure to use all the screws in all the openings (I sometimes just use a few to make it easier to undo but with a fawn, you need all of them in place).

I consider cloth/fabric type crates as not only insufficient for holding a fawn, but they can lead to serious injury, even death. A fawn can tear through a soft sided carrier. A deer's legs or neck can get hung with crates that have metal framework inside. They are also next to impossible to keep clean. Kennels made entirely of wire are very dangerous as well. Fawns can get a foot through and break a leg. They're also uncomfortable.

The rehabilitation room should not be air conditioned, but kept a comfortable temperature. Fans may be necessary to keep the air circulating. On hot days in the wild, deer have options for cooling down such as moving to a more comfortable area, taking advantage of a nice breeze, finding a shady spot, or cooling off in a pond. These options aren't available to a fawn in a carrier so make sure the room does not get too warm or oppressive.

This room should be well away from areas of human activity so fawns are not exposed to talking, television, or other decidedly human noises. The rehab room should also be away from the smell, sight, and sound of dogs. Otherwise, fawns will either stay constantly frightened or grow accustomed to dogs and have no fear of them once released. Either scenario is bad.

The room should not be overly bright. You do not want to keep it dark (except at night, of course), but less lighting makes things less stressful. Although not critical, it is nice to have a nature sound machine in the room to imitate some of what the fawn would be hearing in the wild. I keep one in all my indoor rehab rooms/buildings and on a sunny day, I play birds singing. On rainy days, I turn it to the sound of rain and at night, I switch it to crickets, frogs and other evening symphonies.

Speaking of nature sounds, I recommend not talking "human" to fawns. Trust me, I know how hard it is to avoid, especially baby talk. You want to tell them what a "cutie, sweetie precious widdle baby" they are, but it is better to speak their language, not ours. So as funny as it may sound, I bleat or make the soft mewling sound the mother would use to "talk" to her babies.   Try it and watch how they turn their head and look at you.   It is also helpful in quieting a frightened fawn.   I do sometimes wonder what it is I'm saying in deer dialect.   I certainly hope I'm not using foul language by mistake!   I also wonder if the fawns ask themselves - "who does this human think she's fooling?"   But I do mimic (as best I can) what the mother would sound like, be it a deer, squirrel, raccoon, bear, or whatever. Some species I do a better imitation of than others, I must admit!

Outdoor housing

Older fawns should be kept outdoors in a fenced area at least six feet tall.   Fencing should be stockade-type boards, wooden panels or chain-link.   Wood fencing should have one plank butted up to the next with almost no space between (other than what is necessary for expansion of the wood on warm, humid days) or a fawn can get a leg or head caught.   You would be amazed at what tiny spaces a fawn can get jammed into!

With chain-link, interior walls should be lined with shade cloth (see Supplies & Where to Find Them – pg. 22) to at least 4 ft. high.   This will serve as a visual barrier and help preclude a fawn from getting caught in the chain link.   If fawns get spooked and begin running into the fence, the cloth will prevent them from slamming directly into the wire. The chain link has some "give" so deer aren't crashing into a solid surface, which is why I personally prefer it to wooden fencing.   It also allows for better air flow.   Fencing should absolutely not be made of barbed wire, chicken wire, or any other type of wire as these can be extremely dangerous to a panicked fawn.   They are also insufficient in so many ways.

What size pen you need depends on many things.   How many fawns will you be caring for? Will you have more than one pen?   Will the pen open out into a fenced pasture or, once the pen door is opened, are the fawns no longer enclosed?   Minimum pen size is 10 x 20 x 6 feet high, but the overall size truly depends on the circumstances.   If you have several pens and only a few fawns per season, then a 10 x 20 x 6 is sufficient.   If you have only one pen and take in a lot of fawns per season, then obviously a much larger enclosure is required. Since time in the pen is limited and neither long-term nor permanent, however, the space does not need to be as big as it would if they were in there a long while.   Deer should have room to walk, play, eat, sleep, and use the bathroom, and enough space so those activities can be separate (i.e. you don't want the fawns eating in the space they use the bathroom in or sleeping in the space they eat).   They do not necessarily need a lot of room to run, though. They can do plenty of that once released and if they are able to build up too much speed in their pen, they could end up getting hurt.

The pen should be placed in an area away from dog and human activity (visually and audibly.)   The exact configuration of the pen is up to you, but should contain the following:

a. shelter for the grain feeder

b. shelter for the fawns

c. water container

d. visual barrier

e. hiding places for the fawns

f. an appropriate "floor"

g. a top on the pen (not critical, but preferable).

details of above recommendations:

a. Grain molds easily so it must be kept out of the weather.   If it gets damp, it also attracts insects which lead to larva in the grain. You can either build a small shelter to keep the grain dry (be sure the fawns can easily get to the food) or the grain feeder can be placed under the shelter you build for the fawns themselves.   The former is the far better choice because regardless of how clean you keep things, the food will attract "unwanteds" and having them in the deer's sleeping/lounging area is undesirable.   Once grain gets even slightly damp, it has to be thrown away.   For that reason, I recommend only putting out a small amount at a time, at least until the fawns begin eating it regularly and in large quantities.

b. Fawns require a dry, comfortable place to sleep.   They need to get out of the rain, wind, and sun when necessary, yet have access to fresh air, sun...even rain... when desired.   The configuration is limited only by your imagination, but you need to be sure it is safe.   There should be no gaps for hooves or heads to get caught in.   There should also not be any spaces between the shelter and the sides of the pen for fawns to get trapped.   I am always stunned at what tiny spaces they get caught in.   For our fawns, we created a manger of sorts.   It has a wooden floor (with pine shavings on top for comfort), a solid wood back, and one side pressed into a corner of the pen, in effect creating a side wall.   The other side is open, however, making it easy for fawns to enter and exit by either the front or side.   This keeps them from feeling too hemmed in as deer are very claustrophobic.

c. Any open containers of water should have a way for small mammals to escape if they fall in. Not only is it a horrendous death, but a dead animal in the water is not healthy for the fawns either! Just be sure the escape feature does not interfere with the fawns being able to drink, does not leech any dangerous substance into the water, and isn't something the fawns will get tangled in. (We use faux lily pads that float on top the water.)

d. You can use either shade cloth or wood fencing. As mentioned, shade cloth allows for better air flow and lets some light in, but reduces what the fawns can see outside the pen. Wood fencing totally bars deer from seeing outside the pen. The choice is yours, though I prefer shade cloth.

e. Cut down some lush trees and pile them up for the fawns to get behind or under. Though deer are claustrophobic, they also do not like to feel exposed or out in the open. Although evergreen trees stay green longer and have to be replaced less often, I prefer leafed-out deciduous trees. Cedar trees are prickly and pines have sticky sap that is next to impossible to remove from fur.

   (_Personal anecdote_: _it took years to convince management that lack of hiding places for the fawns was not natural and, therefore, stressful. They felt shade cloth was sufficient. However, the enclosure was quite large and I believed the fawns needed to feel less exposed. Finally, they put cut trees in a corner area of the pen. The first time I went in after this was done, I panicked. I thought someone had left a gate open and all the fawns had escaped because there wasn't a single one in sight. I soon found them all hiding among and behind the brush pile!_)

f. If the ground has grass or groundcover thickly covering it, nothing more is required. If the soil is bare, rain (combined with sharp hooves) can quickly turn it into a mud pit, so pine shavings should cover it. Do not use hay, cedar shavings, gravel, or concrete. Hay tends to hold moisture and develop potentially dangerous molds. Once it's saturated with moisture or urine and begins decaying, it becomes a wet, heavy, slimy mess that is difficult to rake up. Cedar shavings have a strong scent disliked by fawns. Gravel and concrete can create hoof and leg problems, and are typically chilly, uncomfortable surfaces to stand or lie on.

   Whether pine shavings are necessary depends on the soil in your area, how compact it is, how well the area drains, and how large the pen is. If it is a large pen and certain areas begin to show more erosion than others due to "high traffic," you can place cut trees in those vicinities, forcing fawns to make another path elsewhere.   If the pen size does not allow this luxury, then pine shavings will be a necessity.

g. A top will prevent other wildlife from entering the facility in search of food or looking to harm the fawns.   It can be chain link or wire.   It should be secure enough to keep out raccoons or opossums.   Flimsy wire could easily bend under their weight.   The top does not need to be as heavy-duty as the sides, however.   Since raccoons can get into places you wouldn't dream possible, the top and sides should be securely attached to each other, leaving no gaps for a clever raccoon to get through. All portions of the top should be high enough that a jumping fawn won't snare his neck.   It is doubtful you will keep out all creatures.   Mice are attracted to the grain and snakes are attracted to the mice.   In addition, things like wasps, hornets, or bees can become a problem.   Your goal is to keep out what you can, and handle what you cannot.

Note: Do not use barbed wire for the top (or any part) of the fawn pen.   Although fawns cannot dig out of their pen, there are animals that can dig in, such as feral dogs and coyotes. If such animals are a problem in your area, you will need to bury wire along the bottom of the pen to keep them out.   Any rehabber who has had dogs or coyotes get to their fawns can attest to the nightmare it is.   Not only do they tend to kill every single baby, but typically tear them to shreds in the process.   It is a horrific scene to come upon and one you never forget…or forgive yourself for.   (I'm fortunate this particular situation has never happened to me.   However, there have been other, equally horrible, situations.   Although I can credit myself with only making a mistake once, if anything happens to my patients while in my care I feel tremendous guilt, both then and forevermore.   It does not matter that I'm human and there is no way to predict every potential risk.   I am the "mommy" and while an animal is in my care, I am responsible for his welfare.)

where to locate the pen
Where to place the pen on your property will depend on many factors.   What other species are you caring for and where are those pens located?   How large is your property?   If you have outdoor dogs, where is their enclosure?   How close is the nearest road?

How large your property should be to properly care for and soft release fawns depends on the size of the properties surrounding you, as well as how close the nearest deer hunter resides or hunts.   Whether you are for or against hunting is not the issue.   You certainly don't want to put the time, money, and energy into this only to have the fawns be easy prey for people one property over.   If, for example, everyone in your area has hundreds of acres, they all welcome (or at least tolerate) deer, and are okay with what you are doing, then your having only a few acres is not a problem.   However, ideally you should have at least ten acres and the properties around yours should all be at least that size as well (and bigger is much better).

Deer need a large area and cannot be properly rehabilitated or released in neighborhoods, subdivisions, near businesses, etc., even if deer have been spotted in such areas.   When I created the fawn program around soft release, lots of people applied that did not have a good location for raising and freeing fawns.   Perhaps they lived on a single acre, were near a busy street, were renting their home, raised hunting dogs, or resided near a business.   One example, people lived in a subdivision with one or two of the lots wooded.   They could not understand why their home wasn't a good rehab spot, after all there were trees.   However, deer need more than a tiny "island" of woods to survive.   There is also no way to open the gate and the deer magically gravitate to that particular land mass while completely shunning the neighbors' yards.   In addition, while those one or two lots may be wooded today, tomorrow the bulldozer may arrive and a new house go up.

Deer need enough acreage, privacy, and space to be raised away from people, have plenty of room to wander, explore, find food and water, raise their young, i.e. live a full deer life once released.   They need enough land to avoid being run off or harassed by existing deer herds, dogs, and humans.

Rehabbers new at caring for fawns may think if there are a lot of deer on their property, it's an ideal location to raise and release more.   However, land can only sustain so many deer, so if your property already has a lot of them, then it is not suitable for more since existing herds will continue to grow, as will the newly released ones.   There is much to consider before deciding if your land is appropriate for deer rehabilitation.   In addition, while it may work well for a few years, you may get to the place where adding any more deer will be detrimental to all of them.

The fawn pen should be well away from the house, garage, backyard, workshop (i.e. away from the sight, sounds, and smells of humans and pets), but within sight so you can keep an eye out for intruders, feral dogs, etc.   The only way you could get by with it being out of eye/earshot is if you have an alarm system that alerts you to a problem, one that sounds inside the house and not at the pen itself as that would terrify the fawns!

Quarantine and misc. recommendations

Any fawn that comes in should be quarantined for three days. After quarantine is over, if there is no sign of illness, it is acceptable to put two tiny fawns in one large dog crate as long as each has plenty of room to stand, urinate, move, and lie down. This is for really little fawns only. Otherwise, keep it at one fawn per crate. If you do put more than one fawn in a large crate, bedding must be changed more frequently. (Note: if two fawns arrive together and are very small, they can go through quarantine in one crate since they have already been exposed to each other.)

For very young fawns, you can use sheets, blankets, old t-shirts, etc. for bedding, just nothing they can get their legs tangled in (for example, open-weave knitted afghans would be a bad choice). It is also important the bedding be absorbent, and changed regularly to avoid urine burns and keep the fawn from lying in his own excrement. Fawns can produce an unbelievable amount of urine for their size and no animal wants to sit in their own waste, even for a short period of time. Be vigilant and keep your fawns dry and clean. Once fawns are stabilized, eating well from a bottle, and showing no sign of illness, they should go into the rehab pen.

Since fawns will be soft-released from their enclosure, you need a gate that can be left open to allow deer to come and go (when it's time). You will continue to provide nourishment and water during the soft-release period. (See Release Criteria – pg. 51) As long as the fawn is healthy and it is summertime, soft release can begin at approximately 3 ½ - 4 months of age. They would not be hard released at that age, but since they will continue to be offered food, water, and shelter, this is not too young to begin the process (and it is a process).

If you have some fawns set to begin soft release and others that are not, you will need to either hold back those ready or devise a way to divide the pen to allow soft release to begin with some but not all.

FEEDING INFORMATION:

Formula

Fawns can be bottle fed goat or deer milk replacer.   Some choose to use fresh goat's milk. We have used, and recommend, Purina Kid Milk Replacer.   The choice is up to the individual rehabilitator, but we noticed problems, such as diarrhea, with other brands so we prefer Purina.

Though deer milk replacer is probably superior, it is <u>considerably</u> more expensive than goat's milk replacer.   Since the latter is a close second, most will understandably opt to use that. If you don't take in many fawns per season, the exorbitant cost of fawn milk replacer may not be a problem, but for those that take in a lot of fawns, the expense can add up quickly.

If using deer milk replacer, mix according to package directions.   With goat's milk replacer, mix at 75% what the container indicates for standard goats.

As with other species you are rehabbing, if a fawn comes in dehydrated, you should administer rehydrating fluids first.   Only after the fawn is rehydrated and warm should you begin formula.   If the fawn is emaciated, been without food for several days, or given the wrong milk by the public, you should dilute the formula and work your way up to full strength to avoid taxing the digestive system (just as you would do with other mammals). By the same token, you don't want to take too long working up to full strength on an emaciated deer since he is already dealing with malnutrition issues.

At no time should you use any form of cow's milk, cow's milk replacer, or formula containing medications and/or antibiotics.   Using drugs without reason is damaging to a fawn's GI system.   Antibiotics cannot discriminate between good and bad bacteria, so they destroy both.   Our intestinal systems rely on bacteria to properly function, but is even more critical in ruminants.

Do not use a formula designed for multiple unrelated species even if it indicates it is also safe for deer or goats.   Use one specifically formulated for goats or fawns.   Given how different each species' milk is, I have to wonder if a formula that claims to be good for everything can really be good for anything?

<u>Note</u>:   Purina goat milk replacer comes in an 8 lb. bucket (white with red lid, at least as of this printing).   However, they also have it with Decoquinate added to prevent coccidoisis. That comes in a 50 lb. bag.   I do <u>not</u> recommend the medicated version.

Purina makes a formula called ProNurse Milk Replacer that they recommend for a wide variety of animals, including white-tailed deer.   I have no experience with this product, but a deer rehabber I have great faith in has used it and her deer had diarrhea while on it. However, since Purina does recommend it for white-tailed deer, I would be interested in hearing from anyone who has tried it for fawns, especially someone who has used other products and can compare them.

Bottle & nipple

Fawns can be fed using a Pritchard lamb's nipple, soft lamb's nipple, or crosscut <u>juice</u> nipple (human baby-bottle type).   The latter is available in most grocery or department stores. You will need the kind designed for older babies.   They fit regular (human) baby bottles that utilize a screw-on cap.   (<u>Note</u>: you will likely need to enlarge the crosscut on the human-type and possibly the lamb's style.)   A preemie or regular nipple will not work. They are too soft and will collapse under the fawn's strong suckling.   A fawn suckles vehemently and if he gets frustrated, will quit trying.   Do not use a calf nipple.   It is much too large.   Each rehabilitator has their own preference and should use what best suits their fawns.   (I used human baby-bottle nipples with my fawns and had no problem, but others swear by the Pritchard or lamb's nipples.)

When you are first teaching a fawn to suckle from a bottle, start with a "soft" bottle, one you can squeeze and cause formula to come out the nipple. Once a fawn learns to use a bottle, switch to a non-flexible, rigid type because they suckle so hard, they end up collapsing a soft one!

Bottles should be glass or sterilizable plastic.   Do not use plastic soft drink or water bottles. They are not designed for reuse and can leech chemicals into the formula.   They will also not stand up to temperatures high enough to thoroughly clean.   Juice nipples go on a human baby bottle.   With lamb or Pritchard's, you can use a glass bottle or one designed to work with such nipples.

Bottle training

Fawns need to be bottle trained, not given formula out of a bucket or bowl.   It is rare that a fawn will readily latch on and suckle from a bottle since it looks, smells, and tastes nothing like mom; it will have to be taught.

Be prepared for a struggle.   An occasional fawn will take hold and drink right off the bat. More often than not, it is not an easy process and must be done carefully to avoid injury to you and the fawn.   In the early stages, you may end up with more formula <u>on</u> you than <u>in</u> him, but before long, the little one will get the hang of things.

Generally the best method is to further dim the lights in the rehab room.   Have a warmed bottle of formula prepared and ready.   Put a quilt on the floor to sit on.   Wrap the fawn in another quilt leaving only his neck and head free.   Sit on the floor with the fawn between your legs, his head facing away from your body and his rump pressed tightly into your abdomen area (the fawn should be in a seated position during the initial training period). You may need to press your legs into his sides to keep him from struggling and thrashing, firmly but <u>gently</u>!

With your non-dominant hand (the left for most of us so I will refer to it as the left for simplicity sake), pry open the deer's mouth and with your other hand, insert the nipple.   The fawn's head should be slightly tilted back so the neck is elongated.   Using the palm of your left hand under his chin, keep his head tilted.   Squeeze a small amount of formula into his mouth.   Use your left hand to hold the fawn's muzzle closed (do not cover the nostrils). Continue to squeeze formula into his mouth and watch (or feel) for him to swallow.   <u>As long as he is swallowing</u>, continue to squeeze in more formula.   Using the hand holding his muzzle, squeeze his mouth shut, then loosen, squeeze it shut, then loosen.   Keep on with the squeeze/release in a rapid motion to manually simulate suckling.

<u>Note</u>:   As silly as it may sound, if you have a dog that is easy to get along with, practice the proper positioning and head tilt with him.   It won't be the same as a struggling fawn, of course, but will give you a feel for things anyway.

If the fawn becomes stressed, let him rest a few minutes before trying again.   You may have to work with him like this for several feedings before he will take any amount worth noting. After trying for a little while, put him back in his carrier, even if he did not drink much.   He is not (typically) going to learn in one feeding, or even two or three, so the longer you push him at each feeding, the more stressed you and he will become.   I assure you, once he learns, the formula will disappear rapidly!

Once a fawn becomes used to the bottle, let him stand to eat.   He may still need you to open his mouth to insert the nipple, but once latched on, will suckle without assistance.   Let him step out of his crate to eat, but be sure the floor is not one he will slip on.   If it is, put down a non-skid rug or something he can safely stand on.

While the fawn is out of his crate, this is a good opportunity to change the bedding.   After some experience, you should be able to feed the fawn with one hand and change bedding with the other.   Oh, and be prepared, he may choose to eliminate while he is out of the crate.   Putting a washable "pee pad" down on top of the non-skid rug is a good idea.   (The disposable types are too fragile for a fawn's hooves.)   Sometimes fawns will wait until they are back in their nice clean crate to use the bathroom.   That's always frustrating, but understandable.   After all, we prefer a clean potty, too, right?   If it happens, just count to ten, take the fawn back out of the crate, remove the soiled bedding and try again.   Just wait until he's finished or you'll end up doing it a third time!

For a fawn that comes in a couple months old and is extremely wild, do not risk injury to yourself or the deer by forcing him to bottle feed.   He can drink from a bowl or go straight to solids as needed.

If a fawn arrives badly injured and stressed, syringe or bowl feeding to avoid further stress or injury is okay.   He can be taught to bottle feed in a few days when he is more stable.   Just don't put it off too long because he is much easier to bottle train the younger he is.

Why bottle feeding is important

I have always believed suckling fulfills important psychological needs for mammals.   It is very comforting to a little one.   Some species even require a pacifier between feedings (raccoons and black bear cubs are two that do).   Though fawns don't need one, suckling is as comforting to them as any mammal.

In addition to the comfort factor, however, for fawns there is a physical need for suckling. Deer have four-chambered stomachs.   The first (and eventually largest) chamber is the rumen.   However, it is not functional when a fawn is first born.   In the beginning, the abomasum is larger than the other chambers and this is where formula is shunted for digestion.   It is not a direct route from the throat (esophagus) to the abomasum so formula must bypass the rumen.   To do that, a special groove forms when a fawn suckles that guides milk into the proper chamber.   What causes the channel to "open" are a number of factors, including a natural nursing position (neck extended, head tilted slightly back), the expectation of nursing (the fawn realizing formula is coming), and the taste of formula in his mouth.

If formula ends up in the rumen (which is where it will go if the esophageal groove isn't open), it can, at best, slow digestion and absorption.   At worst it can lead to severe (possibly fatal) problems.   Therefore tube feeding should be an absolute last resort in a fawn less than three weeks old.   If a fawn is too weak to suckle, it may still be able to swallow so syringe feeding would be the way to go.   If he cannot swallow, sub-Q or IV fluids would still be preferable to tube feeding.   After the fawn is older and the rumen properly developed, tube feeding is less dangerous, though still should be a last, not first, choice. Tube feeding should only be used when other feeding methods have failed or are impractical, and then for the shortest time possible. There are situations when it is necessary (a veterinarian can determine what those situations are), but should never be employed simply to make things go faster and easier for the rehabilitator.

Bottle (vs. bowl) feeding is also more sanitary. An open bowl can be stepped in, soiled in, and/or tipped over, and then a mess ensues. Spilled formula can become a breeding ground for bacteria and will attract insects.

Only one individual should be feeding the fawns, particularly in the early stages of care when there is more hands-on. Later, when the fawns are older and more skittish, a second person can be added IF ABSOLUTELY NECESSARY, but <u>never</u> should more than two different people (total) <u>ever</u> feed or tend to fawns to be returned to the wild. Fawns easily imprint on humans, more so than most wild species. With squirrels, opossums and the like, an imprint means a neighborhood pest and people can be bitten or otherwise injured. With imprinted deer, however, you are looking at much more than a nuisance. People can get seriously injured, even killed (see Deer Physiology - author's note - pg. 140).

It is unavoidable for fawns to become accustomed (even attached) to the caregiver. I personally believe that is okay as long as (a) it's only one person and (b) that person treats the fawns as close to how the real mom would as humanly possible. It is critical fawns not become accustomed to humans in general. If there is one caregiver from beginning to release and that caregiver follows certain guidelines, then the fawns should not become imprinted. Granted it's a lot of work for one person, but it is what's best for the fawns. Other people can help with tasks that don't involve contact, such as mixing formula, cutting browse, washing cloth bedding, etc.

<u>Bottle racks/multi-feeders</u>

Once fawns are outdoors and eating well from bottles, they should be switched to a bottle rack system or bucket (lamb) feeder (see Supplies & Where to Find Them -pg. 20). Doing so reduces the contact you have with the fawns.

You can devise a rack to work with either a chain link or solid wood pen and bottles can be loaded (and unloaded) from the outside. How many fawns you typically take in will determine how many racks and spaces you need. Racks should be different heights so fawns can reach them without having to either stretch or hunch down. The holes must be drilled in such a way that the bottle tilts downwards.   Otherwise fawns won't be able to get all the formula out.

With a bucket system (special buckets that hold formula and have nipples encircling them), hang them at various heights.   Buckets must be higher than the fawns so they drink with their necks in the proper outstretched position, but they should not have to strain to reach the nipple.

Some rehabilitators go so far as to purchase deer targets (life-size realistic-looking plastic "deer" designed for hunters to target practice on) and hang the bucket feeder in front near where udders would naturally be.   I think it's a nice idea for those that can afford it (or ask someone to donate them.   I rarely get donations of any kind, but it doesn't hurt to ask!)   If you are using a rack system, you could get someone who's good at art to paint a wooden cutout to look like a doe, then cut holes for the bottles along the middle.   A fake doe is certainly not critical to rehabilitating fawns, but anything that mimics nature is a plus.

Solid foods

Fawns should be offered goat chow on a continual basis, though typically only older fawns will eat it.   Do not use feed formulated for horses, cattle, or any species other than goats (or deer fawns).   Do not use a goat chow that contains medications!   Check the grain regularly to be sure there is no mold, moisture, or insects in the bottom where you can't see.

We used (and prefer) Purina Goat Chow (#5501).   However, Purina makes a number of goat chows, so be sure you get the correct one.   You do not want Purina Show Chow Goat Ration (#55F5), Purina Meat Goat 16 DQ (#55U7), or Purina Goat Mineral (#5509).   You need to be especially mindful of Purina Meat Goat 16 DQ because the bag looks identical to Purina Goat Chow!   Meat Goat 16 DQ contains Decoquinate.   As with the formula, I do not recommend one with medication.

If your feed store has to order the grain, be sure to give them the full name and number of the feed you want, then double-check before signing for the order.   If you're in a hurry, it's easy to glance at the bag and assume it's the right one since the two bags look the same.

Fresh browse should be offered to young fawns at least once per day.   Older fawns should have unlimited access to browse.   Remember, deer are primarily browsers, not grazers. Therefore having access to only ground-level plants will not suffice.

Deer have four chambered stomachs (see Deer Physiology - digestive system on pg. 135), but when a fawn is born, only the abomasum is functional.   Browse (vines such as honeysuckle, grape, and trumpet; leaves such as maple, sassafras, and gum) is crucial to the development of the other chambers. You will need to experiment to see what your fawns will eat since plant life varies by area of the state or country. If your pen does not naturally provide unlimited access to browse, you will need to gather it several times a day, every day. It does not stay crisp and fresh long once cut, particularly in the warm weather months.

You may be amazed at how much browse a small herd of fawns will consume each day. Pay attention to what browse the fawns are and are not eating so you can provide a good variety of what they like. You do not need to give them just leaves; they will eat the small, green stems as well. It is very important that deer get a mixture, just as they would in the wild. If they are given a single type of browse, even if it is a good quality and large quantity, deer will develop health issues after just a couple weeks.

If you do not have a cover on your pen, you can toss the browse over the top rather than going in. This will reduce your interaction with the fawns. Do not give them greens purchased at a grocery store. You will be wasting your money as they quickly wilt and deer typically won't eat them.

You may notice fawns nibbling on dirt at times. This is perfectly normal and should not be discouraged. If dirt is not accessible, provide a small pan of it. Use "every day" dirt you'd find around your property, not potting soil or soil that has been fertilized or treated with chemicals.

Deer should have access to clean water at all times. They cannot convert dry food into water as some animals can, so they require water year-round. Young deer need more water per pound than adults. Much comes from the leaves they eat, as well as dew or rain that forms on vegetation. Although deer can get fluids from eating snow (or licking ice), it takes a lot of energy to thaw and should never be used as their source of water (for example, if you have to winter over fawns).

Misc. feeding information

Sterile conditions are neither feasible nor desirable when tending to fawns. Like humans, they need exposure to various everyday germs in order to build a proper immune system. However, common sense cleanliness is important. Sick fawns should be cared for after healthy ones to avoid transmitting disease on your clothing. Sick fawns should be isolated from your healthy herd. Wash your hands before and after working with fawns.

Formula should be mixed before each feeding (mix in a pitcher or bucket, depending on the number of fawns in your care.   You do not have to mix each bottle individually).   Bottles should be rinsed after each feeding and disinfected once a day.   You can run them through a dishwasher (top rack), wash in disinfectant (such as white vinegar or bleach), or boil them. (Fawns that are sick need to have their bottles disinfected after each feeding.)

Fawns are notorious for "bottle switching" - pushing each other off their bottle and latching on to several different ones during the course of a feeding.   This is impossible to prevent (short of feeding them individually) and is perfectly okay.   After all, they are in the same pen and groom each other regularly anyway.

If, for some reason, you need to disinfect a pen, you can use white vinegar at full strength. It is a potent natural disinfectant that kills bacteria, viruses, and fungus without the toxic problems you get with other choices.

Feeding schedule

Fawns 0 - 2 weeks of age: 5 bottle feedings a day.

Fawns 2 - 4 weeks of age: 4 bottle feedings a day.

Fawns 4 - 10 weeks of age: 3 bottle feedings a day.

As fawns reach 10 weeks of age, they can gradually be weaned to two bottles, then one, then one every other day, etc.   By the time soft release begins at 3 ½ - 4 months, they may still be wanting (and receiving) a bottle feeding or two a day, but should be eating primarily grain and browse.   In the wild, they are weaned at five months.   The mother doesn't just go from a lot of nursings a day to none, however.   She gradually weans them.   Again, you are mimicking what the mom would be doing.

Keep in mind, the feeding table (above) is a general guideline, not a hard and fast rule. Fawns that come in thin and malnourished may need more bottle feedings than their age dictates.   I always feed based on their "size age" rather than their chronological age.

Note that "a bottle feeding" does not necessarily mean one bottle.   Some fawns, depending on the size bottle you are using, may consume more than one per feeding, particularly when older.   A fawn will drink vigorously and, at first, you will wonder if he is going to drink until he explodes!   Then suddenly, he stops cold.   When fawns are finished, they are finished - they don't want any more.   It is rare to have a fawn overeat.   Unlike raccoons and black bear cubs who will drink formula until it comes out their nose (and still want more!), fawns tend to stop once full.   Some species, like squirrels, are inclined to slow down and then quit, but fawns go from full throttle to dead stop with nothing in between! They suckle so vehemently, white foam appears around their mouths.   This is normal. They also yank on the nipple and butt the bottle, sometimes so forcefully they knock it out of your hand or the rack.   This is what they would be doing to their mother's udder if she were still around.   After observing this, you cannot help but feel sorry for mama deer!

Note: Fawns are notorious for suckling on your earlobe, neck, leg, whatever they can grab hold of.   They also have an uncanny ability to seek out the spot on a female caregiver they would look for on their mother, so beware what you wear and how you bend over, or you could find out the hard way just how sorry you should feel for a mother deer!   Fawns are anything but gentle.   Even if it is through clothing, it still hurts!   Some fawns also "nibble" on your clothes and legs and, again, can get quite aggressive about it.   They are not trying to hurt you, but it can be painful nonetheless.

If you have a fawn that overeats, you need to watch and take the bottle away before that happens because bloat can be a serious problem.   In all my years of doing this and "tons" of fawns I've cared for, I only had one that tended to eat too much, but she did not develop bloat ...just a well-rounded tummy after a feeding!   The only deer I had with bloat was one that had been down and not moving.   It is frightening how rapidly bloat forms and how serious it can quickly become.

Always provide enough bottles and time so every fawn gets a chance to eat.   This is particularly important when fawns are feeding from a bottle rack or bucket system.   You need to be sure the more assertive fawns are not preventing smaller, shyer fawns from eating. Once everyone has their fill, you can remove the bottles.   There should always be formula left over so you know everyone got what they wanted.

Do not dispose of excess formula on the ground.   It will sour and smell, breed bacteria, and attract bugs.   Pour it down the sink when you get back to the house.

Foods to avoid

In addition to the foods mentioned in this chapter, it is fine to give fawns (older than 4 weeks) an occasional slice of apple or little bit of watermelon as a treat, just not in large quantities.   Deer should not be given dried corn.   Many rehabilitators (and the public) see "deer corn" at feed stores and assume it is good to feed deer, a reasonable assumption. However, deer corn gets its name, not from the fact it's healthy for deer, but because it's what hunters use to attract them.

43

Deer will eat large quantities of corn, so between the name and the way deer gobble it up, people think this is a good food for them.   However, it is not.   First, deer will over eat corn, meaning they are filling up on that instead of foods they should be eating.   Second, dried corn is heavy and tends to sink to the bottom of the rumen, ferment, and cause bloat.

Deer should not be given bread, table scraps, or sweets.   Deer are vegetarians and their digestive system is not designed for meat.   To avoid serious GI distress, as well as malnutrition, it is important to stick with the proper foods.

Foods for wintered-over fawns

Fawns that arrive in late summer or early fall will need to be wintered over and soft released in the spring.   The care information is basically the same, with a few differences.

When a fawn is born late in the season, it will have a baby (spring) coat.   Whether there will be enough time to change to a winter coat before cold weather will remain to be seen. The fawn should be kept outdoors as the weather begins to cool to help the coat molt to a winter one.   However, if it does not, special precautions need to be taken when really cold weather arrives.   The deer will need a heated place to sleep (such as an outdoor heating pad) or access to a warm barn on particularly cold days.   You don't want to create "summertime" temperatures for the fawn as that will only further confuse things when it comes to molting, but without the fortification of a winter coat in cold weather, they will need assistance to get through the really low temps.

In order for the digestive tract to properly develop, a deer must eat vegetation.   However, for fall babies, access to leaves won't last long.   Once the four chambers are properly functioning, the deer will need to switch to a winter diet.   They should be given the grain discussed above, as well as acorns (known as "hard mast").   This is in addition to their formula, of course.

Note: At our facility, we hold an annual "nut drive," where we ask people to gather acorns for our winter-over patients.   This way we have fewer nuts to purchase (and let me tell you, nuts are very expensive in the quantities we use), plus the deer are eating what they would be getting in the wild since they find and consume far more acorns than, say, pecans, walnuts or almonds.

It is important acorns be properly collected, as well as correctly stored, or they will go bad. They should be accumulated on a dry day after it has been dry for several days.   They should be put in paper bags or cardboard boxes, never plastic bags or containers, and stored in a dry area away from weather and rodents.   Acorns should be collected while firm and solid.   Avoid any that are lightweight, have mildew, are "powdery," or are dried up.

URINATION AND DEFECATION

In young fawns consuming primarily formula, feces should be formed but soft and have little odor.   If the stool is watery; gray, green, or mustard yellow in color; contains blood or mucous; and/or has a foul smell, there is a problem.

As fawns get older and grain and browse are added to their diet, stools should be small dark brown (almost black) pellets, similar to what a rabbit produces, only larger.   Sometimes the pellets are sticky and therefore form a single stool, but the individual pellets are still recognizable.

It is not unusual for a fawn's urine to have a strong, distinct odor, particularly as he gets older.   It isn't unpleasant (at least I don't think so), but is definitely discernible.   Once you've smelled it, you'll recognize it from thereon out.   After you've grown accustomed to what it should smell like, you can ascertain unusual odors that might indicate a problem.

A tiny fawn temporarily housed in a large dog crate must have the bedding changed frequently because he will produce a large quantity of urine.   If not kept clean, his fur will stay wet and can result in urine burns.

You may sometimes notice fawns standing in an odd position to urinate, holding their back legs together in a strange manner, then rubbing them together as urine runs down the legs. This is normal behavior and has to do with "scenting" (see Deer Physiology - scent glands on pg. 134).

Fawns may attempt to nurse on each others genitals.   This is not common, but is also not rare.   It typically does not create a problem unless a fawn has diarrhea, then the "nursing" fawn can end up with a mess on his face!   If that occurs, you need to clean him up before it dries, if possible.   Otherwise it becomes extremely difficult to remove.   Other than that, genitalia nursing is rarely a big deal.   However, if one fawn badgers another to the point of making the genitals sore, red, or raw, then you may have to separate them, at least temporarily, to break this habit.

Sometimes the "nursing" fawn will actually drink some of the urine that results from the stimulation.   Again, this is no cause for concern unless it gets out of hand.   (Personal note: in my many years of doing this work, I have never had to separate fawns for this reason.)

Some sources state very young fawns need to be stimulated to urinate and defecate.   I have taken in fawns literally from birth (delivered via C-section) and have NEVER had to stimulate one to eliminate.   I don't mean rarely, I mean never.

SUPPLEMENTS

Colostrum

Colostrum is the thick, yellowish substance the doe produces the first three days after her fawns are born. This "pre-milk" is very nutritious and quite important to the fawns' development. It contains antibodies that protect little ones from illness and disease. Fawns who do not receive colostrum have a much slimmer chance of survival. With some colostrum, even if not the full three days worth, his chances increase.

A fawn must receive colostrum immediately after birth to do what it should. Antibodies in colostrum are large celled. There are (to put it in simplistic terms) large openings in the body for the antibodies to pass through. These openings shrink as the doe's milk changes from colostrum to milk. If the fawn is away from the mom any length of time during that period, the "openings" will close prematurely and there is no reopening them. Colostrum given after that point is not properly absorbed. Once the opportunity is lost, it is lost for good. Unfortunately, by the time the public, animal control, wildlife officer, or whoever gets a fawn to a deer rehabber, usually too much time has passed and the chance to administer colostrum is gone. If you are not sure, it won't hurt to give colostrum. It may do some good, it may not, but it won't hurt.

When a fawn is delivered via C-section or "born" when the mother is hit by a car, it is important to start him on colostrum immediately (see Supplies & Where to Find Them on pg. 17). You can use powdered or fresh goat colostrum. Keeping colostrum from a local goat dairy in your freezer prevents you trying to find some at the last moment. Just thaw as you need it.

Mineral Licks

There is debate whether rehabbed fawns need a mineral or salt block. I am not convinced they need either, but if you are going to use one, choose the mineral block.

Keep in mind when it rains, minerals will leech into the soil so keep far from ponds, lakes, wells, creeks, and other sources of ground water. In addition, the minerals can damage nearby trees, shrubs and flowers so don't put anywhere near favorite plants!

Misc.

As a general rule, there is no need to give fawns supplements. There are plenty of nutrients in the formula, goat chow, and leaves the fawns will be taking in. If a fawn is recovering from an illness or injury then supplements may be needed, but not typically on a day-to-day basis.

RELEASE CRITERIA

<u>When to begin the process</u>

Exactly when to begin the release of a fawn is up to the rehabber. With soft releases, fawns can be let out of their pens at a younger age than with a hard release because they will still have access to the enclosure, as well as food and water, for a period of time.

You can begin soft-release at around 3 1/2 - 4 months if they are spring babies. In the past in North Carolina, nearly all fawns were born in May like clockwork. Today in our state (as well as others), fawns are born at various times of year, not just spring. This rarely happened when the male-female ratio was more balanced (see Deer Physiology - Reproduction on pg. 139).

If you have spring babies of different ages, you can either hold back the older fawns while waiting for the younger ones to reach release age, or house them in separate pens and begin release at different times. If there are only two fawns, hold the older one back because at no time do you want a single fawn if you can help it. Having at least one other fawn reduces the risk of imprinting.

<u>Once release begins</u>

No one, except the original caregiver, should have been approaching the fawns during their rehabilitation process. This remains an important rule during soft release, as well. If a fawn moves toward someone other than the caregiver, that person should clap their hands, shout, and make an effort to scare away the fawn. I know it is not easy and they will feel like an ogre doing so, but it's best for the fawn. Fawns not afraid of people (or dogs) may end up killing or getting killed. Deer without fear of humans become dangerous as they get older, particularly the males and especially during mating season. That is why it is crucial fawns be raised to fear humans and dogs. It is a disservice to remove that fear, yet is very easy to do. Fawns imprint easily and, because they are so cute, you find yourself wanting to pet or talk to them, then wanting to share that experience with others. In a word, **DON'T!!!** You may wonder how letting the kids pet them just once or having a few caretakers rather than one is a big deal, but with lots of experience, I can assure you it is hard enough to raise non-imprinted fawns when you follow all the rules, impossible when you don't.

If you want to share these beautiful creatures with others (and who can blame you, they are darling), use a camera. But do not allow anyone other than yourself (and if absolutely necessary, a second caregiver) anywhere near the fawns. Remember, deer have a much better sense of smell, sight, and hearing than you do so letting the kids (or others) stand at a distance and watch you feed counts as contact! The fawns will know they have a human audience.

If semi-tame deer begin showing up in your area, and animal control or wildlife personnel are called in to handle these "problems," there is a chance you could lose your permit (if your state works on a permit system). You could potentially be sued, particularly if someone is injured by an imprinted fawn you raised. So it is in everyone's best interest to raise fawns to live a wild existence.

After you open the gate to begin soft release, do not push the fawns to leave the pen. Let them do so at their own pace, when they are comfortable. Continue to keep the grain feeder filled, as well as the water bucket. If the fawns are still getting a bottle (and most likely they will be), you can put bottles in the rack at their normal feeding time and let them have formula if they so desire.

It is preferable to offer a bottle at a given time each day vs. racing off to prepare one whenever a little one shows up. Not only will you run yourself ragged, but it will teach the fawn that regardless of when he shows up, "mommy" will have a bottle for him. This is during a time when he should be learning, instead, to rely less on you and more on himself. Also, if you have numerous fawns, it can be confusing keeping up with which fawns showed up that day and got a bottle and which did not.

Some fawns will continue to return to the pen off and on during the day to eat, sleep, or take a bottle. In the beginning, it is not unusual for them to hang close to the pen and, when you're around, to you. As time goes on, the fawns will venture further and further and return to the pen less and less. At first, you may see them repeatedly during the day. Later, you may see them once a day, then every few days, then once in a while. As they gain confidence in their newfound freedom, you may eventually go weeks without seeing them, thinking they are gone for good only to have them show up for a brief appearance before disappearing again. As they gain their independence, let them do just that. Do not encourage them to return to the pen, though it is okay if they do so on their own. In other words, there is no reason to discourage them either.

Some deer, particularly those raised in a relatively small rehab pen, may panic the first few times they step outside their previous confines into the big world. It is frightening for them. It is also upsetting to the caregiver to see them so distraught. The fawns may run around in circles, obviously scared. You feel very helpless at a time like that. To make it less problematic, make sure there are buckets of water outside the pen for them to stop and drink from; be sure to open the gate for the first time on an overcast day when it isn't overly hot (deer do not fare well in warm weather); stay where the fawns can see you, calling softly to them in whatever manner you used with them as newborns; and open the gate early in the morning while it is still cool.

Hard release vs. soft release

If you are considering a hard release with fawns, I hope you reconsider. I have seen releases done both ways and I can tell you, a soft release is <u>by far</u> the better way to go. If fawns are old enough to survive on their own without back up care, then they are big enough and wild enough (or should be!) to cause serious injury to you and themselves during the capture process. Even when handled by professionals (wildlife officials who have a lot of experience handling fawns), deer have ended up with broken necks (i.e. killed) during the roundup process. The deer panic and start running full tilt into the fence until they either escape, knock themselves unconscious, or kill themselves.

Once the deer are put in a proper trailer for transport, they must then endure the ride to wherever you plan to release them. You get there, open the door, and they come flying out into an area they are completely unfamiliar with and with no back up food. Studies have shown only a tiny fraction of hard-released rehabilitated fawns survive. Most die in a short period of time.

If you absolutely intend to do a hard release in spite of this advice, then you should never release before they are five or six months old. They should never be hard released during winter months. If at all possible, hire a professional to round up the fawns and transport in an appropriate trailer (not in a crate, car, SUV, etc.) Back up food should be provided until the fawns are well established in their new area. Fawns should be released in the general area/climate they were found. As an example, although deer in the mountain area of our state are the same species as deer in the coastal region, you would never release deer from the mountains at the coast or vice versa.

Soft releasing fall babies

Fall babies need to be wintered over. When they are the normal age for beginning soft release, it will be the middle of cold weather and not an appropriate time to let them go. With wintered-over fawns, you can start soft-release in the spring once trees begin to leaf out. By that time, they (and you!) will be more than ready to start the process.

<u>Note:</u>   See Feeding Information - foods for wintered-over fawns on pg. 44.

<u>Identifying or marking fawns</u>

When fawns are very small and you are bottle feeding them numerous times per day, more than likely you can identify which fawn is which.   As they get older and contact diminishes, telling one from the other may be more difficult.

There are many "tried and failed" methods of marking fawns.   Each one we tested at the state facility had its pitfalls.   Some failed miserably, while others worked very short term. We found no good, temporary method, which is what we were looking for.   In our case, we only needed to keep track of how fawns from one area of the state fared compared to another.   When released, however, there could be no identifying marks per state policy.

Whether fawns can or should be permanently marked will vary so know your state's policies. Keep in mind in this day and age, people sue right and left.   If someone is involved in an automobile accident with one of "your" deer and he is traced back to you, there is no guarantee the person won't claim the deer ran into the road because he was tame.   Even if completely untrue (after all, deer are hit by cars all the time and the majority were not rehab patients), you will still need to defend yourself in court.   Court costs, even if you win, can prove astronomical, not to mention the negative publicity it can cause your wildlife center. I suggest not marking fawns.   Of course if someone (public or rehabber) improperly imprints a fawn, then releases him into the wild where he later hurts someone, they <u>should</u> be held accountable.   I am concerned, though, about people out for an easy buck (pun intended) by claiming a tagged deer did damage somehow.

Never put a dog collar on a deer, even temporarily.   I cannot tell you how many times we've gotten calls about deer with embedded collars.   The deer were obviously hand raised (usually illegally) and had gotten too big or dangerous for the person to handle, so they released him.   They don't want him shot or injured though, so they use a collar to let hunters and others know it was/is a "pet."

Not only will the deer grow as he gets older, but during rut, a buck's neck swells tremendously (see Deer Physiology – reproduction on pg. 139).   A collar will cause serious problems and should never be used, even if you intend to remove it before release.   You have no way of assuring the deer won't escape and once that happens, he is free with a collar around his neck!   Then what?

If you do need to temporarily mark a fawn for some reason, check into the olefin tags you mark on with permanent markers.   (See Supplies & Where to Find them - pg. 20 under Jeffers).   Remove as soon as the need is over and certainly prior to release.

COMMON AILMENTS:

A word about antibiotics

Antibiotics should only be used when medically necessary. They are generally contraindicated for G.I. ailments such as simple diarrhea, salmonella, and e. coli. Using antibiotics for these type ailments typically extends the time the organism is shed, as well as destroys beneficial bacteria in the G.I. tract. Treatment should, instead, consist of good supportive care, hydration, and treating the diarrhea (see below).

When antibiotics are indicated, such as with animal bites or broken bones (particularly compound fractures), it is important the entire course be administered, even if the animal appears better sooner. Giving a partial course may kill off the weaker bacteria but leave the stronger behind. The resilient, surviving bacteria can then build up a resistance to antibiotics, resulting in a "super bug." If the resistant bacteria is transmitted to other fawns, even though they themselves did not take antibiotics, it complicates treatment for those infected from there on out.

If you stop after a partial course and the condition starts getting worse again, do not use the same antibiotic because, at that point, it may not work. (Note: if a deer has a bad reaction to an antibiotic, stop administering and contact your veterinarian immediately so he can prescribe a different type.)

After a course of antibiotics, beneficial bacteria to replace those killed by the medication is crucial. Beneficial bacteria is found in yogurt that contains "live cultures" or probiotics (comes in capsules, powder, or gel). One we recommend is Ultimate 10 Probiotic from the Vitamin Shoppe (see Supplies & Where to Find them on pg. 21).

Beneficial bacteria is normally destroyed by excess heat, so it should be added to a bottle after it has been warmed and started to cool down, or else given separately. (You can put it in a little white grape juice and administer with a syringe.)

Given the billions of microorganisms in a deer's digestive tract (see Deer Physiology - digestive system on pg. 135), it would be best to use probiotics vs. yogurt because most yogurts contain limited types of good bacteria (usually acidophilus) whereas probiotics contain a variety.

There is some debate as to the best time to add back good bacteria. Some start immediately. If the deer gets antibiotics at noon and midnight, for example, they administer probiotics halfway between doses, at 6 a.m. and 6 p.m. Others argue the added good bacteria will be wiped out so it is a waste of time and money prior to the completion of antibiotics.   For me, it depends on how long a course the animal will be on as to when I start.   If it's a short course - say 3 days - I usually start the day before the antibiotics end.   If it's a longer course, I start about three days before the course ends.   If it's an exceptionally long course, I give probiotics every other day throughout the entire period, then twice a day for a week after the last dose of antibiotics.

There is no harm starting probiotics during the course of antibiotics, though they will be destroyed.   By the same token, I'm hoping by putting back some good bacteria, even if it does get wiped out, it might hold off a really nasty bacteria from taking over, one the current antibiotic doesn't treat.

The bottom line is it's completely up to you.   You can start at the beginning, follow my guidelines, wait until the antibiotics are gone, or something in between.   The critical part is to give them and not wait any longer than the last dose of antibiotics.   Otherwise you leave the door open for some really nasty "bugs" to move in.

Diarrhea

If a fawn comes into your facility with diarrhea, or develops it after arrival, add 2 tablespoons of a kaolin-pectin anti-diarrhea medication (see Supplies & Where to Find Them - pg. 20) to the fawn's formula.   Do NOT use Immodium, Kaopectate, or similar anti-diarrhea medicines.   These may stop diarrhea but tend to keep toxins in the intestinal tract, allowing them to reproduce and cause further problems.   Kaolin-pectin, on the other hand, absorbs toxins yet allows their departure from the body.   The only time it is okay to use an anti-diarrhea medicine like Immodium is when diarrhea is undoubtedly dietary in nature, e.g. from the fawn being fed cow's milk.   If not absolutely sure, use kaolin-pectin.

The most crucial issue with diarrhea is replacement of fluids _and_ electrolytes. If diarrhea is severe, replace formula with fruit flavored rehydrating fluid (such as Pedialyte) mixed with a high energy supplement (I recommend Nutridrench) for 24 hours, or mix formula with unflavored rehydrating fluids instead of water for a few feedings. This can be done in addition to the kaolin-pectin. You may also wish to try a product called Ultimate Fiber by Nature's Secret (see Supplies & Where to Find Them - pg.21).   It comes in powder form and must be refrigerated. You mix it in the fawn's bottle, then feed it to him immediately. The product becomes gelatinous fairly fast, so don't let it sit around.

An herb well known for healing GI problems is slippery elm bark (see Nature's Medicine Cabinet on pg. 107).   Purchase in capsule (powder) form and either mix in the fawn's bottle

58

or mix with white grape juice and administer with a syringe.   It is one of the ingredients in Ultimate Fiber (above) and becomes gelatinous quickly, so don't let it sit around long after mixing.

Exact dosages are not critical when dealing with herbs, which is one reason I prefer them to prescription medicines.   However, a dosage guideline is listed under "List of herbs" beginning on pg. 94.

Blood and/or mucous in diarrhea is cause for concern.   It typically indicates the mucosal lining that protects the intestines is shedding.   Slippery elm bark or Ultimate Fiber is important because it helps coat and heal the damaged intestines.   Do not skip doses.   You can contact your veterinarian to see if he has further advice.   He may want to test the feces to see what you are dealing with.

Note: Kaopectate used to be kaolin-pectin, thus the name.   However, this is no longer the case.   Kaopectate is now the same type formulation as Immodium.

Avoid antibiotics for diarrhea unless it can be determined through a fecal culture that the diarrhea is bacterial in nature AND a type that should be treated with antibiotics.   As noted, follow with a course of beneficial bacteria whether the antibiotics are taken orally or injected.

Generally speaking, e. coli, salmonella, rotavirus, etc. are quickly fatal, even with the best care.   They are also typically very contagious and you could end up with your entire herd sick.   This is why it is so important to quarantine new arrivals and feed/tend to healthy deer before the sick ones.   If you are dealing with a disease, like e. coli, you should not only thoroughly wash your hands, use separate feeding instruments, and keep the animals in separate areas, but change your clothes after working with the fawns, as well.

(Personal anecdote: I learned the hard way about clothes.   I took ALL necessary precautions except that.   When my outdoor healthy fawns came down with the same e. coli two indoor fawns were battling, I scrutinized everything and realized the only possibility was my clothing.   It broke my heart to know I was responsible.   I am not perfect, I make mistakes, but I learn from them and don't make them a second time.   Still, that is little consolation for the first go-round.)

It took a lot of experience, but I've gotten to where I can tell e. coli, salmonella and rotavirus by the smell and look of the diarrhea.   However, it isn't something you learn overnight.   You have to deal with a lot of cases before you can discern the difference, and then only if you have a very sensitive nose.   The differences are actually pretty subtle.

From my observations, e. coli is painful for deer. The fawn starts with severe diarrhea, which progresses to containing blood and mucous. After that, it is only blood and mucous being excreted. Then you see the fawn hunched, as though having a bowel movement, but nothing is coming out. They strain and are obviously in pain. I believe in treating pain regardless of cause, so have your vet give them medication to help.

I have treated e. coli two ways - with traditional medicines and with natural. None of the fawns survived with traditional medicines. I saved some with natural methods, but frankly, not many. E. coli is tough. Salmonella and rotavirus are both daunting, too, though I have successfully pulled more fawns through with those than e. coli.

Bloat

Any deer that develops "bloat" needs immediate attention. Bloat occurs when a deer fails to expel gas in the rumen. It can be caused by change in diet, over-feeding certain foods (such as corn), a sick deer lying on his side, etc. Bloat can be fatal, not to mention painful, so early treatment is critical. An ounce or less of peanut, corn, or soybean oil can be given as a drench. Another option is poloxalene (brand name - Therabloat.) One teaspoon of baking soda to four ounces of water can cure a mild case of bloat. Simethicone (brand name - DiGel) can also be effective. Massaging the sides and keeping the animal upright and moving will help. A severe case may require inserting a feeding tube through the mouth into the rumen to release gas.

Another type of bloat that occurs in very young fawns is called abomasal bloat. It is even more dangerous than bloat in the rumen and more rapidly fatal.

Note: After extensive rains, certain plants can become problematic for cattle, horses, goats, etc., making them quite ill and sometimes proving fatal. After hearing from numerous rehabbers I was training about fawns suddenly developing bloat (and many dying), I wondered if it could be due to this. We did have a lot of rain that season. You may want to add Therabloat (or similar product) to the bottles any time there is a lot of rain to hopefully circumvent bloat. If you have several cases (vs. a single incident), pay attention whether there has been a lot of rain. Plants most affected are pasture plants (alfalfa, clover, graze cereal crops, forage rape, and young grass) so take care to give fawns only browse (plants that grow above ground level). Cattle seem more susceptible to bloat from this than other ruminants, but some individuals are more likely to bloat than others, and it is difficult to predict which are and which are not.

Misc.

Worming fawns is neither recommended nor necessary.   Certain parasites are normal in deer (see Parasites/Pest Control on pg. 81).   Fawns being rehabilitated for eventual release should not receive vaccines, such as rabies, distemper, etc.   (As stated in "From the Author," the information in this book is geared toward rehabilitating fawns, not permanent captive situations.   Deer not being released may require vaccines.   Check with your state for this information.   It is beyond the scope of this book to provide information on permanent captives.)

Note: As a general rule, medications safe for goats are safe for fawns.   They are very similar physiologically.

COMMON INJURIES

The decision to euthanize a fawn for injuries is a highly personal one. Some states dictate which fawns are euthanized. If yours does not get involved in these decisions, it is up to you and should be a case-by-case assessment. If you choose to work with an injured fawn, it should be at least possible that the fawn can be released at a future date (unless your state allows deer to be kept as permanent captives). A deer does not have to be "perfect" to be releasable. One-eyed deer, three-legged deer, etc. have been successfully returned to the wild. The main criteria is - does this animal have a good chance of surviving and living a quality existence? To release one with a low chance of survival or that will have to struggle to exist is inhumane. There must be more to it than getting the deer to live at any cost.

At the other extreme, I have seen rehabilitators euthanize fawns with a high chance of recovery. They didn't want to put the work into getting rid of maggots or cleaning wounds. The smell and mess that goes along with severe diarrhea was more than they wanted to deal with or the extra medical treatment required with certain conditions was too much for them. They basically wanted kidnap victims...clean, healthy fawns that just needed a bottle every so many hours. That is **not** rehabilitation. It's foster mothering. Rehabilitation involves illness, injuries, nasty smells, blood, maggots, and some pretty "non-Kodak" moments. If you are only interested in fawns without injuries or illness, you may want to reassess your decision to be a deer rehabilitator because the majority that come in are in bad shape. Perhaps, instead, you can work as a surrogate mom at your local zoo or humane society. Those positions are important, too, and don't involve the gory stuff.

Fawns come in with a wide array of injuries. Some of the more commonly seen are: dog attacks; farming equipment accidents; automobile accidents; capture myopathy; intentional shootings; fawns caught in fencing; and fawns trapped inside a fenced area. Although each situation must be evaluated on a case-by-case basis, there are certain injuries generally seen with each.

Transporting a sick, injured or orphaned fawn

Very young fawns usually travel peacefully in a car. However, for safety reasons, they should not be allowed to ride unconfined. Fawns should be placed in a dog crate (see Indoor Housing for Young Fawns - pg. 27) lined with soft bedding (anything the fawn can't get his hooves caught in). Do not use hay or leaves due to the risk of toxic mold.

When fawns are a little older (over two or three weeks of age), handling them without injury to you and/or the fawn can be difficult. He may be small, thin, and have "toothpick" legs, but don't underestimate his strength or how badly he can hurt you (or himself). The legs are quite powerful. If held incorrectly, a fawn can gyrate his rear legs so violently you think your shoulder will dislocate (I refer to it as the "washing machine" move). The hooves are also very sharp even if they don't look it.

A fawn should never be held longer than necessary. The crate should be carried to where the fawn is rather than the other way around. Fawns should not be carried upside down or placed on their back. They should also never be "hog tied."

If the fawn is small enough to be handled, hold him firmly against your body in an upright position. Use your prominent hand to hold the back legs gently outstretched near the feet. This greatly lessens the amount of kick and gyrating they can do. The other arm should be under the deer's chest.

Never use a catch pole or rope on a deer. Not only do you risk breaking their neck, but if they get away, they are dragging a noose. Not good!

If the fawn is too big or "wild" to be picked up and carried, he may have to be sedated for transport. Under no circumstances chase a deer any length of time, even if you are trying to help him. He will eventually collapse from exhaustion and you can subsequently pick him up, but then you are dealing with capture myopathy, so what have you gained? You can try for a minute to see if catching the fawn is do-able. If not, stop the chase before you do more harm than good.

When you have the fawn safely in a crate inside your car, cover the front with a sheet. Keep the radio off during the drive to your facility. Sick and injured animals lose their ability to properly thermoregulate. Therefore, do not run the air conditioner. Two exceptions are if it is sweltering, in which case keep it on a cool, not cold, setting and not blowing directly on the fawn. Second, if a fawn has suffered a heatstroke or heat exhaustion, he will need to be cooled down.

Dog attacks

With dog attacks, tiny fawns are often grabbed and shaken, which can result in a broken or injured spine, injured or broken neck, internal bleeding, head trauma (as in "shaken baby syndrome"), crushed ribs, punctured lung(s), and/or puncture wounds.

Dogs are also notorious for grabbing a fawn at the rear and biting/tearing at this softer area. The extent of the damage usually depends on how quickly intervention occurred. If someone stopped the attack rapidly, the area may "only" have endured severe bites. If the attack was not stopped quickly, the fawn may be alive but missing vital parts. The only humane treatment in that case is euthanasia as the fawn will not recover.

(Personal anecdote: We were brought a fawn dogs had gotten to. The person calling was an EMT who insisted the deer could be saved because "there is no arterial bleed." When we got the fawn to our facility, we were stunned. A good portion of the hindquarters was missing. There was no way to tell if he was male or female because the genitalia were gone. Most of the kidneys were destroyed, some of the intestines were eaten, the rectum was no longer there, and the bladder was non existent. How this man thought the fawn was salvageable is beyond me, especially him being an EMT. My husband said he didn't know if he hoped this guy never comes to his aid during an emergency (because he didn't appear to know much) or if he hopes he does (since he obviously doesn't easily give up on a patient)! As you probably figured out, the fawn did not survive.)

Unless bites are extremely superficial, antibiotics are recommended (see Veterinary Advice - treatment protocols - pg. 87) Wounds should be thoroughly cleaned with sterile saline, tea rinse (see Nature's Medicine Cabinet - pg. 91) or Nolvason (see Veterinary Advice - pg. 88). Do not use sterile <u>water</u> as it stings, nor hydrogen peroxide as it is damaging to tissue. Do not put Neosporin on bite wounds as this tends to "seal in" bacteria.

I highly recommend garlic oil on wounds (see Nature's Medicine Cabinet - pg. 101) as it kills bacteria, viruses, and fungus, without sealing the wound like ointments do. I have cleared up some incredibly nasty infections with garlic oil. It has a strong smell, but it works wonders. Of course do not use it near the eyes or on extremely delicate areas, such as the genitals. Otherwise, it's safe to use just about anywhere and can be used on even deep wounds. The base is olive oil. It does not burn or sting. Another benefit - flies avoid wounds treated with it. I sometimes use it on uninfected wounds just to prevent flies from laying eggs on the area.

Fawns old enough to run are typically chased by dogs and may or may not suffer an actual attack. However, even if the dog/s does not catch the deer, the fawn can still die from capture myopathy. (see pg. 68)

<u>Note</u>: In addition to dogs, fawns can be attacked by other predators (see Deer Physiology - predators on pg. 129). The injuries differ in some ways (such as where the most damage

occurs), but in general you would treat the same as dog attacks. Dogs harm or kill more fawns than all other predators <u>combined</u>.

Farming accidents

Very young fawns will remain where the doe placed them, even when danger approaches. Though they may look around when things are quiet, as soon as a person or other danger nears, they lower their head and stay perfectly still in an effort to blend with the surroundings and not be seen. This defense works great in most situations, but not if a fawn has been left amid high grasses slated for mowing. When machinery goes through to cut hay, fawns are often unnoticed until too late. Some are killed instantly. Others die soon thereafter. Many suffer severe cuts; some lose parts of their legs. Whether they can be rehabilitated depends on the severity of the injuries.

(Personal anecdote: We were brought the most precious little fawn who had a run-in with a harvester. Three of her legs were cut off at the midway point. "Other than that," she was in perfect health. I cleaned the wounds, bandaged her legs, and covered them with pretty pink vet-wrap. Seeing her all curled up, soft, clean, and beautiful, I tried to figure out how we could amputate the fourth leg and have her survive as a very short deer. But I knew the reality was she had to be euthanized and it broke my heart.)

Automobile accidents

As incredible as it sounds, over a million wild animals are killed on our nation's highways <u>every</u> day! This does not include those <u>injured</u> daily, too. Many are deer. Fawns following their mother across the road are sometimes hit by a car. The extent of the injuries depends on where the fawn was hit, what size vehicle was involved, and how fast the car was going. However, as you can imagine, any time you pit a vehicle against a deer, especially a baby, the animal comes out the loser.

Injuries to the fawn should be assessed, then the decision made whether to treat or euthanize. Typically the deer suffers broken bones, in addition to internal injuries. It is rare a deer is hit in such a way that he "only" has a single broken leg, although the public will often argue that's all that's wrong.

Occasionally a deer is clipped by the car and sent tumbling, resulting in bruising and "road rash." These injuries sometimes appear worse than they are. Wounds should be thoroughly cleaned using Novalsan, sterile saline or black tea rinse. Then, since no bite is involved, cover the area with a topical ointment such as Neosporin, aloe vera gel, or vitamin E ointment to keep the area moist while it heals and to help prevent infection. If the deer is being kept outdoors, use garlic oil to keep away flies.

If the person calling is who hit the deer (or witnessed him being hit), gather as much information as you can. What part of the deer was hit (head, rear, or middle)? Approximately what speed was the car going? What type of car was it (tiny VW bug or big SUV)? Did the deer go down immediately? What was his behavior after the accident (standing but going in circles? unconscious? conscious but unable to get up?) Although you cannot rely solely on this information, it should help you focus your examination.

If you suspect internal bleeding, give the fawn a small amount of cayenne pepper in white grape juice. It is a natural old-time remedy to stop internal bleeding and is surprisingly effective (see Nature's Medicine Cabinet on pg. 91). If unsure whether there's any internal bleeding, treat anyway. It won't hurt anything and could be very beneficial.

X-rays will help locate any broken bones. Your vet can then discuss how many breaks there are, where they are located, how bad they are, and whether the injuries are fixable in such a way the fawn can get up and down during the recovery period. A ruminant down for a long period of time usually develops serious (often fatal) problems, so it is a crucial issue when deciding whether to treat or euthanize.

Once a broken bone is properly set, horsetail (herb) will help it heal much faster. In fact, the herb works so rapidly you should not start until it the break has been set or it could begin healing in an incorrect position. (See List of herbs - pg. 102 for more details).

Consider with broken bones or any serious injury how much one-on-one care the fawn will require, as well as how many trips to the vet's office will be needed and the length of stay while there. A vet's office is not only filled with people (the vet, vet techs, office staff, and clients) but dogs as well. Even if the vet takes great care to keep the fawn away from dogs, the deer will still hear them. If a fawn requires a lengthy recovery process with a lot of human contact, especially if the care involves many visits to the vet's office, the fawn is likely to imprint. This makes a future release difficult, if not impossible. Before devoting the time, money, and love required, consider if it is the right thing to do.

Note: The two times a year deer are most often hit by cars are during rut season and shortly before a doe gives birth when she becomes very territorial.

Capture myopathy

Any time a deer is chased, whether by dogs or well-meaning humans, it can potentially create serious physical problems referred to as capture myopathy. The sooner this is treated, the greater likelihood the animal will recover. Even still, it is unlikely the deer will make it.

The public rarely understands that even if their dog did not actually get hold of a deer, damage from being chased in and of itself can be fatal. People do the same with young fawns old enough to be mobile but too little (at least in their opinion) to be on their own. They see a fawn alone and chase him to exhaustion. They believe they are doing the right thing, then do not understand why the fawn dies shortly thereafter.

Without going into a great deal of medical detail, the extreme exertion sets off a complex chain of events including increased respiratory and heart rates, muscle stiffness, fever, and damage to internal organs. Deer build up excess lactic acid that the kidneys have trouble clearing. Some deer die soon after the chase. Others may hang on for 24-48 hours before succumbing. The deer is typically lethargic, weak, has pale gums and is often unable to sit up. His urine is usually a rusty red or brown color. He can typically swallow any fluids or medication you syringe into his mouth, but is rarely able to suckle.

The deer should be cared for as soon as possible. Keep him calm. If he's not sitting sternally, prop him so that he is. There is no treatment, per se, for capture myopathy; you treat the symptoms. This can be done by a veterinarian (See Veterinarian Care - Treatment Protocol on pg. 87). You can utilize some (or all) of the following natural treatments on your own. Or you can do both. If the latter, let your vet know what you used and how much before he begins treatment.

Even with prompt therapy, there is still a good chance the fawn will die. Chances of survival without treatment, however, are somewhere between slim and none.

To help flush toxins	Choose one: • Lactated Ringers Solution via syringe, IV or sub-Q • oral rehydrating fluids (such as Pedialyte or Gatorade) via syringe
For shock	Choose one: • Rescue Remedy (homeopathic tincture) • hydrangea (herb) • gotu kola (herb) • oatstraw (homeopathic tincture) • Nutridrench (liquid supplement)

To bring down fever & help with pain	Choose one: • ibuprofen (short term) • burdock root (herb) • butcher's broom (herb)
To flush the urinary tract	Choose one: • uva ursi (herb) • buchu (herb) • couch grass (herb)
For healing, especially white muscle disease which often results from being chased	Use both: • vitamin E (supplement) • selenium (supplement)
For muscle cramping	Choose one: • cramp bark (herb) • blue cohosh (herb) • dong quai (herb) • lobelia (herbs) • valerian root (herb)
For glucose	Choose one or both: • Nutridrench (liquid supplement) • apple juice via syringe
To regulate heart rate	Choose one or both: • hawthorne berries (herb) • Rescue Remedy (homeopathic tincture)

Caught in fencing

A deer ensnared in a fence expends tremendous effort to free himself. He usually suffers cuts and abrasions that become filled with dirt from repeatedly thrashing on the ground. Depending on how the deer is caught, there is often a dislocated or broken leg. Another major concern is capture myopathy (see above). Even though the deer wasn't chased, the intense struggle often produces the same results.

A dislocation, like a broken bone, has a limited timeframe to be properly repaired. If the injuries are not fixable, the deer should be euthanized. If you feel the injuries are repairable, treat for capture myopathy as quickly as possible, then tend to the injuries immediately thereafter.

Intentional shootings

When I first started rehabilitating deer, I fully anticipated taking in a lot of wounded (as in gunshots or bow and arrow injuries). It has turned out we've had very few and, in fact, none were from hunters but people shooting them for pure cruelty. Whether hunters are good shots and kill vs. wounding or whether wounded deer die deep in the woods before anyone can find and help them, I'm unsure.   I only know we rarely received wounded deer and none as a result of hunting.

If you are brought a deer with an arrow lodged in his body, it will be critical to keep him still.   That may require sedation.   If the deer thrashes around, it could push the arrow further in or off to one side, causing a lot more damage than has already been done.   Do not attempt to remove the arrow yourself.   Those sharp barbs will do more damage coming out than going in.   Also, depending on where the arrow is located, removing it could cause hemorrhaging.   This type of injury needs to be handled by a veterinarian.

The same thing goes with a gunshot.   A vet can determine where the bullet is lodged, whether it can be safely removed, if the deer is better off leaving the bullet where it is, or if he should be humanely euthanized.

Note: If a deer has been shot out of season or shot as an act of "vandalism," you should report the incident to your state's wildlife officials.   They will let you know what they need – records, vet report, x-rays, perhaps even the deer's body should he not survive.

Trapped inside fenced-in area

Deer that get into a fenced-in area and cannot get out will repeatedly ram the fence in a frantic effort to escape.   It usually isn't that the deer can't get out, it's that he panics and cannot find his way out.   If he got in on his own, he can theoretically get out, but when frightened, tends to bounce off the fence instead of jumping over it or exiting through a gate. The first time you witness this behavior, it is very frightening (so is the second, third and fourth time, as well).

Injuries typically seen are: broken neck, neck compression, skin and muscles torn away from the lower jaw, injured eyes, concussion, broken jaw, exhaustion and/or capture myopathy. If the deer is not severely injured, the gate can be opened and the deer gently corralled toward it.   However, if there are injuries to the jaw, eyes, neck, or back, the deer should either be euthanized or treated (depending on the severity), not released.   If the deer is too large to treat, it is more humane to euthanize than release him into the wild with severe injuries.

Note: Sometimes a deer will have babies inside a fenced area.   In that case, the fawns cannot get out because they aren't yet old enough to scale the fence.

DEER DISEASES

It would be impractical within the confines of this book to cover every aspect of every disease white-tailed deer can contract.   However, the following is a good overview. Diseases are listed in alphabetical order.   Some are extremely rare, others more commonplace. You should have a basic understanding of even the rarer ones so you can answer the public's questions, or in case you are actually faced with the disease.

Anthrax

Rare in the United States.   It progresses rapidly, often killing animals within hours.   Fever, problems breathing, weakness, and loss of blood through body openings are common symptoms.   Clinical signs in white-tailed deer have not been documented, but are assumed similar to other herbivores.

Anthrax is caused by swiftly-multiplying bacteria that spread throughout the body. Herbivores (cattle, sheep, ruminants, horses) are most susceptible, but dog, cats, swine, and humans can also be infected.

Soil is the reservoir.   Warm temperatures or major shifts in the soil's moisture level (heavy rains or drought, for example) can cause the bacteria to multiply.   Animals ingest the anthrax while grazing or eating dirt.   Once infected, the bacteria can spread to others via biting flies or mechanical means.

Outbreaks in white-tailed deer are infrequent, but the death rate can be extensive when it does occur.

In humans, most cases are skin infections from anthrax entering a scratch or wound.   An abscess, followed by secondary blood poisoning, may occur.   Exposure can result from people handling carcasses, meat, bones, or hides from infected animals.   Infection through inhalation or ingestion is very rare, but can be quickly fatal as we learned from terrorist attacks in the early 2000's.   (For more information on anthrax and humans, visit the CDC's website.)

Blackleg and Malignant Edema

Caused by anaerobic bacteria in the soil (same genus as Clostridium). Either can result in bleeding under the skin (subcutaneous hemorrhage) and build-up of fluids (edema). White-tailed deer of any age can contract the diseases. Given hemorrhagic disease can lead to secondary issues with blackleg or malignant edema, it can be unclear which is the actual cause of death, but is most likely the former. Both are diseases of livestock and deer are sometimes blamed by farmers or ranchers, but when it occurs in cattle, sheep, and the like, deer are not considered to be the reservoir.

Bovine Tuberculosis

A chronic, progressive disease resulting in pea-sized nodules in the chest cavity and/or lungs. Emaciation, weakness, coughing, discharge from the nose, and problems breathing follow. Sometimes lymph nodes in the neck area will abscess and rupture, draining through the skin.

Bovine tuberculosis (TB) can infect a wide range of mammals, including cattle, elk, bison, deer and various zoo animals, as well as coyotes, feral swine, cats, and dogs. Though captive deer can develop TB, it isn't often seen in wild deer. (In recent years, it has shown up in wild white-tailed deer in Michigan.)

Although wild animals can contract bovine tuberculosis, it does not seem to create significant problems. However, the fear is wildlife will become carriers and spread the disease to cattle (or other domestic ruminants). The United States began a program in 1917 to eradicate bovine TB. Since then, it has been wiped out in most states. Were it to flare up again, it could cause major problems for those who raise (or eat) beef.

Transmission occurs when organisms are ingested or inhaled, then cast off in discharge from the nose, mouth or draining abscesses. It can also be shed in feces, urine or mother's milk. Food and water can then end up becoming a source of infection.

Humans can contract TB, though it is not usually bovine. That is not to say they can't contract the bovine form, just that it is extremely rare. Persons with weakened immune systems are most at risk.

Bovine Viral Diarrhea

Cattle are the primary reservoir of this illness, though sheep can also become infected. This disease is not a major problem for white-tailed deer. However, farmers are very familiar with it and may contact you to ask if deer can make their cows sick.

Brain Abscess

Caused by any number of bacteria. Deer typically have neurological manifestations, such as circling and problems with coordination. These symptoms are also seen with head-injured or poisoned deer so it isn't easy to distinguish by symptoms alone. Brain abscesses are infrequent so in a deer with the above listed symptoms, head trauma is the more likely suspect.

Abscesses are more common in bucks than does; this is probably associated with damage to the antler pedicel which the does, of course, rarely have. Abscesses can become quite sizeable, infecting up to 25% of the brain. Deer with brain abscesses are considered unsuitable for human consumption.

Brucellosis

White-tailed deer have been blamed for spreading brucellosis to cattle. However, repeated studies show deer are not a problem. All cervids are capable of contracting brucellosis, but it's usually only seen in captive elk or bison, even then it is rare.

Abortion during the latter half of pregnancy with babies born weak or dead is a common symptom. The disease is transmitted through the fetus, placenta and vaginal discharge of infected females.

Because brucellosis is so detrimental to the cattle industry, ranchers invest a lot of time, money and energy into regulations and laws resulting in the disease being nearly eradicated in the U.S. In spite of the concern, brucellosis has not been maintained in wild ruminants in North America.

Humans are capable of contracting this disease, although in people it is called undulant fever. It causes joint pain, headache, fever, chills, and other flu-like symptoms (as do many illnesses. Having these symptoms does not mean it must be brucellosis).

Chronic Wasting Disease (CWD)

A neurological disease known as a transmissible spongiform encephalopathy (TSE).   CWD is to cervids what scrapie is to sheep, mad cow disease (bovine spongiform encephalopathy) is to cattle, transmissible mink encephalopathy is to farmed mink and Creutzfeldt-Jakob disease (CJD) is to humans.   All are caused, not by bacteria or virus, but particles known as prions.

The disease brings deterioration to the brain, giving it a sponge-like appearance.   The brain and central nervous system are severely affected.   Symptoms can include salivation, craving excess water, loss of appetite (leading to weight loss and wasting), teeth gnashing, laying around with lowered head and droopy ears, and problems standing or walking.   The disease is fatal.

No one is certain how or when CWD originated.   It was first recognized as an illness in captive mule deer in the 60's, though it wasn't until the 1970's it was pinpointed as a TSE. CWD has been around, therefore, over 40 years and, in that time, has not spread rampantly. That does not mean we can be complacent, however.   CWD can create serious problems for captive and wild herds if it moves into an area.

For more details, and to keep up to date with where CWD is confirmed, check www.cwd-info.org regularly.   You will likely be asked about CWD by the public. There is much misinformation out there, so learn all you can about this disease.   You need to know what to look for.   In addition, the public often comes to wildlife rehabbers with questions so we have a responsibility to have the correct information.

Cutaneous Fibroma

Hairless tumors found on the skin of white-tailed deer.   They are usually temporary and can be found anywhere on the body.   They range from 1/4" to 8" in diameter.   Most are covered with smooth, dark, hairless skin but some can have a rough, wart-like surface. There can be multiple tumors per site, appearing as clumps.   Large fibromas tend to become infected.   Deer to deer transmission may occur with direct contact (or via biting insects). Although unsightly, they are of no major significance. No human infection has been reported.

Dermatophilosis

This unsightly disease is caused by bacteria that can affect both adult and baby deer, though more often fawns.   Patchy hair loss occurs, along with inflammation.   Sores are typically covered with loose, crusty scabs that tend to ooze blood.   They appear most frequently around the muzzle, eyes, and ears, but can be anywhere on the body.   Sores range from just a few to covering much of the body.

Although contagious to other animals and humans through contact, transmission via blood-feeding arthropods (like ticks or biting flies) is also thought to occur.

Treatment with antibiotics is rarely necessary as this disease is self-limiting, typically clearing within two-three weeks on its own.   Medication is used only when sores are extensive and the animal is weak and debilitated with other health issues.

(Author's note: I normally treat the sores with a tea wash (see List of herbs- pg. 96).   The tea is soothing and the tannins help with healing.   I follow with vitamin E oil, aloe vera gel and/or calendula tea (typically I alternate).   If any of the sores become infected, I use garlic oil.)

I cannot speak for other parts of the country, but dermatophilosis is not unusual in North Carolina.   I have taken in many fawns with it.   As for how contagious it is to humans, I have an immune system disorder and am highly susceptible to diseases my patients carry, yet I have never had dermatophilosis.   I handle many, many infected fawns without gloves, but have yet to contract even a mild case.

This disease is contagious to other species, including pets (cats, dogs, etc.).   I cannot tell you how easy or difficult it is for them to contract, however, because I never allow my pets around my wild patients.   I also keep the wild animals separated by species.   Exercise caution and common sense when working with a fawn with dermatophilosis, but luckily it does not appear to be easily transmitted.

Hemorrhagic Disease

In deer, this illness can be caused either by epizootic hemorrhagic disease (EHD) or bluetongue (BT) virus.   Though related, they are genetically distinct.   At present, two serotypes of EHD and five of BT occur in this country.   Six of the seven affect white-tailed deer.   Diagnosis can be made only from a fresh specimen because the virus quickly dies as decomposition begins.   Once the public finds a dead deer and contacts a rehabilitator, it's usually too late to test.

Symptoms change (worsen) as the disease progresses.   At first, deer may have a fever, lethargy, respiratory problems, and swelling of the head, tongue, and neck.   Some die shortly after onset of symptoms, while others linger, becoming emaciated and lame.   Deer are often found dead or dying at the edge of water as they seek relief from the fever.

Visible signs can include ulcerations in the mouth and on the tongue.   There can also be sloughing on the hooves.   Other signs are apparent only upon autopsy/necropsy.

(Author's note: I know the "proper" term is necropsy.   However, I am one of those people who believe animals have rights, feelings, and emotions.   I believe they can suffer pain – both physical and emotional.   I do not believe humans are superior to other species, so I use the term autopsy to make a point.)

EHD or BT are transmitted by biting midges, not from contact.   Humans cannot contract this disease.

Hemorrhagic disease is a significant infectious disease of white-tailed deer.   It occurs annually, more prevalent in late summer when it is warm and humid.   The time of year and the deer being found near water are two clues hemorrhagic disease may be the culprit.

(Author's note: I cannot speak for other parts of the country, but hemorrhagic disease is fairly common in North Carolina, the majority of cases in July and August.)

Infectious Bovine Rhinotracheitis

Affects the respiratory system.   It is a disease primarily of cattle and, therefore, of concern to ranchers and farmers.   However, this illness has not been diagnosed in wild deer.

Leptospirosis

Caused by spirochete bacteria, typically in the urinary tract and spread via urine. Naturally-occurring leptospirosis in white-tailed deer is rare.   Deer exposed to the disease develop antibodies without showing any sign of the disease or shedding the organism.

Malignant Catarrhal Fever

This disease of cattle causes high fever, profuse nasal discharge, inflammation of the nose and mouth, cloudy eyes, and diarrhea. It is not at all common in the United States and not known to be a problem among wild deer. Captive white-tailed deer housed near sheep or wildebeests (for example in zoos) may become infected. If so, they often die suddenly with little sign of illness. When they do exhibit symptoms, it is usually bloody diarrhea, blindness and/or erosive sores in the mouth and muzzle area.

Rabies

All warm-blooded mammals are susceptible to this disease, though some species are more likely than others to contract it. Rabies in deer has been reported, but is rare. Rabies infects nerve tissue, resulting in fatal damage to the brain. It can produce extreme aggression, activity during the day for nocturnal animals (or night for diurnal animals), hydrophobia ("fear" of water), and foaming at the mouth. These are the symptoms most people associate with rabies. However, with "dumb rabies" (which is not another type of rabies, but what can occur if the virus is so virulent it kills the animal before other symptoms appear), you may find the animal lethargic, with partial paralysis, and near death.

You do not have to be bitten to contract rabies. Getting infected saliva into an open cut or sore can transmit the disease. However, the virus is extremely fragile. Even if you are bitten by a known rabid animal and do not receive treatment, chances are low you will contract the virus. However, what makes this disease so frightening is there is no cure - it is a fatal illness. (A person can receive post-exposure inoculations after being exposed to rabies as long as this occurs prior to the start of any symptoms. Once symptoms begin, there is no treatment, other than supportive care. It is crucial that post-exposure treatment begin quickly. If rabies is suspected, injections are usually started before results of the rabies testing are in. If the test comes back negative, no further inoculations are given. If it comes back positive, treatment will already be underway.)

Because rabies is such a dangerous disease (dangerous does not translate to common), many rehabilitators receive pre-exposure rabies inoculations.

If you or the public handles a deer suspected of being rabid, contact the proper authorities immediately (you should know in advance who that is). Testing for rabies is done using brain tissue. Therefore, do not shoot a suspected rabid animal in the head. There is no

77

"live" test for rabies.   The animal must be euthanized for testing to occur.   The body must immediately be kept cool, but not frozen.

(Author's note: To date I have never had a deer I suspected of having rabies.   I have taken in a rabid fox and bat, but those were the only suspected and confirmed cases of rabies I have had at my facility.   When I attended a forum on rabies, there were wildlife officers, biologists, animal control officers, veterinarians, and I present.   The expert teaching the class told us that we were all at risk of being exposed to rabies, but "the person here most at risk is Dana".   I thought that was very startling.   I had gotten my inoculations early on, thankfully, but his comment still surprised me.)

Salmonellosis

This hard-to-treat illness occurs in a wide variety of vertebrates, including birds, reptiles, amphibians, and mammals (including humans).   It is transmitted via fecal-oral contamination (which is easier than one might think) or in contaminated food.   It is characterized by diarrhea, weakness, lethargy, dehydration and, often, death.   The diarrhea is frequently yellow-gray with spots of blood and usually an intensely foul odor.   The illness is treated with good supportive care (see Medications - diarrhea on pg. 90) to prevent dehydration and electrolyte imbalance, which is the primary cause of death with this disease.

(Author's note: I cannot speak for other parts of the country, but I have had several cases of salmonella in fawns here in North Carolina.   It is not as common here, though, as e. coli. Recently, both pet and human foods were recalled due to a particularly toxic form of salmonella.   Animals at our facility were affected.   It was a nightmare.   One of our precious babies died.   Another was left with neurological problems.   It has become terrifying these past few years as nothing appears safe any more.   The tonnage of recalled items is staggering.   The most devastating aspect is the number of people and animals who have died, but we also have to think about all the toxic items being added to our landfills in unheard of quantities.)

Toxoplasmosis

Though white-tailed deer are often exposed, clinical symptoms have not been seen in the wild.   Death is rare.   Toxoplasmosis can be a serious issue in humans, though, and there have been documented cases from eating uncooked, or poorly cooked, venison.   Freezing or properly cooking deer meat will kill toxoplasmosis.

Tularemia

Most of us think of rabbits with this disease, but it can affect other mammals, including humans.   The disease is very rare in white-tailed deer.   Some deer showed antibodies to tularemia, indicating they were exposed at some point but either did not get sick or survived if they did.

In humans, the disease is very serious and can prove fatal if not properly treated.   Fever, swollen lymph nodes, and other flu-like symptoms progress to serious debilitation.   If the disease is properly diagnosed and treated with antibiotics in a timely fashion, most people recover but get quite sick.

Vesicular diseases

Causes sores that look like blisters.   The most notorious is foot and mouth (FMD).   FMD is highly contagious and affects sheep, swine, and cattle.   The mouth, tongue, feet, and teats become covered in painful sores.   Fortunately this illness does not occur in North America. The few times it has entered the country, it was quickly wiped out with potent disinfection and destroying the affected animals (and all those exposed to them).

Another vesicular disease is vesicular stomatitis (VS).   Although rare, it does occur in the United States (as well as Mexico).   Blisters and symptoms are the same as FMD, so testing is required to determine which it is.   Luckily, VS is not nearly as contagious as FMD and does not create the same economic devastation.

Experiments have shown white-tailed deer can contract FMD or VS.   If a deer is found with fluid-filled blisters in the mouth or on the feet, the state veterinarian, Veterinary Services, or USDA should be contacted immediately.   If the deer is alive, he should be restrained and not introduced to further animals.   If he dies, he should be put on ice.   Do not allow anyone untrained in this disease access to the animal.

PARASITES/PEST CONTROL

Abdominal worm

Adult worms live in the abdominal cavity while larvae (microfilariae) circulate in the bloodstream. They do not cause problems for the deer and no one usually realizes they are there unless a hunter discovers them during butchering.

Arterial worm

These "worms" (actually nematodes) occur naturally in white-tailed deer. Adults live in the carotid arteries (or, on occasion, in leg arteries).

The most significant problems they cause (usually in older deer) are loss of teeth, destruction of jaw bones, obstruction of blood flow to the brain, and food impactions in the lower face.

A deer with an oral food impaction is easily recognized. The lower portion of the mouth (what we would call the chin on ourselves) is severely swollen. If you were to open the sublingual space, you would find coarse food materials.

Note: See Veterinary Advice- treatment protocols on pg. 88 for how to treat.

Demodectic mange

The mange is caused by a mite that looks and acts much like demodectic mange in other animals. The deer will lose patches of fur and the skin in those areas will be wrinkled, thickened, and covered in small pustules. Demodectic mange is not often seen in white-tailed deer and typically not a major problem when it is.

Ear mites

The type of ear mite that infests white-tailed deer is also found in mule deer, goats, and domestic rabbits. Some deer have a mild infestation while in others it can be quite debilitating. Excess mites can cause stumbling, problems with coordination, even circling. These are usually from a secondary bacterial infection vs. the mites themselves.

If there are just a few mites, you can only tell with an otoscope. With heavy infestations, the ears are covered in a waxy, scabby, crusty secretion and look very inflamed. Ear mites are contagious.

Flies

When deer are outdoors, they are often bothered by the flies attracted to food, urine, and feces. The enclosure should be kept as clean as possible so flies are kept to a minimum, but even the tidiest pens are going to have problems. I personally do not like any product you put on the deer. If I have to use one, I use an all-natural type. Even those, however, have a strong smell, which is surely irritating to a deer's sensitive nose. Having tried myriad methods of controlling flies, I prefer the Trap N Toss (see Supplies under Jeffers on pg. 20). You put fly attractant and water inside, then hang in the area of concern and dispose of when full.

Take care not to hang the trap anywhere you may accidentally bump it or you will get the most disgusting fluid on you. Even after several showers, you still feel nasty! The attractant itself smells horrid, then add decaying flies to the "soup." Trust me, you do not want this on you so choose your site carefully!

My initial concern was whether the trap would actually draw more flies to the area and make things worse, but if it did, additional pests were rapidly caught.

Large lungworm

Finding lungworms in deer is not unusual. As long as the load is not heavy, deer can live healthy lives. With a large number of these parasites, deer can be underweight and unhealthy, with severe respiratory problems due to excess mucus in the airways.

When there are too many deer in an area, they are forced to eat lower to the ground because they run out of the browse they should be eating. This results in more parasites and can mean the death of much of the herd, particularly the young, old, and weak.

Large stomach worm

Most deer are host to stomach worms without problem. If quantities grow too large, the animal can become thin, unhealthy, and anemic. Usually parasites don't get out of control unless there are other issues, such as too many deer in an area.

Larval tapeworm

Tapeworm larvae tunnel through the intestinal wall, journey through the liver, then attach to the intestines.   The tapeworm does not cause serious issues and are often found in wild and domestic ruminants.   They can be transmitted to canids (dogs, wolves, coyotes), and cause problems for them, but not usually for the deer that carry them.

Lice

There are three types of lice routinely found on white-tailed deer.   As with most lice, these are host specific.

Lice can be difficult to diagnose due to their miniscule size.   Adults lay eggs, then attach them to hairs right next to the skin.   The eggs hatch, then develop to adulthood.

A few lice are not problematic, but if a deer becomes heavily infested their fur looks unkempt.   It tends to fall out in patches and becomes almost powdery.   In general, a deer does not become unhealthy because of lice, rather lice become numerous because the deer is not well.   They may be malnourished, injured, have excessive numbers of parasites, or are old and dying.

Liver fluke

Deer are able to live with a certain number of liver flukes without problem.   They can suffer mild anemia, but as long as deer don't have large numbers, they can live normal, healthy lives.

Louse flies

Four types of louse flies can be found on white-tailed deer and seen when you spread the fur. Some people mistake them for ticks, but louse flies have six legs vs. eight and a three-part body.   What also makes louse flies unmistakable is their swift movement. You see them for a split second before they quickly disappear under another section of fur, moving in an unusual sideways manner.   They are very difficult to remove.

People sometimes refer to them as deer keds.   When an adult lands on a deer it loses the wings.   It remains on the deer, feeding on blood, until it either dies or is forcibly removed.

Maggots & fly eggs

Maggots are a disgusting nuisance rehabbers deal with.   Sometimes they are in a wound and can be flushed out.   However, flies will lay eggs on a weak fawn with no wounds and that is when things get difficult.   The eggs are positioned throughout the fur with the highest concentration along the rump, umbilicus and soft underbelly.   When they hatch, you will be horrified to witness thousands of undulating white worms in the anus, genitalia, and swarming on the underside, especially in the folds of the back legs and lower abdomen.   It takes a very long time, but the maggots can be removed.   The biggest concern are those that enter the subcutaneous tissue through the umbilicus and wreak havoc in places you can't see.

Contrary to what many of us were taught (and some still believe), maggots do not only chomp through infected or necrotic tissue.   They are capable of tunneling through soft, healthy tissue as well.   You can clear all visible maggots only to check an hour later and see small holes not previously there, teeming with more.   If you listen, you can actually hear them inside the fawn's underbelly.   It's horrific.

For external maggots, you can flush them out of a wound with garlic oil or distilled saline.   It's time consuming and disgusting.   You'll feel as if you are covered in them before all is said and done (you probably will have some on you, so you'll want a hot shower after you're finished).   When possible, I do this outside on a big, old sheet I can throw away.   I have tried putting maggots in soapy water (like you do with fleas) and they simply crawl out of the container.   Because they are "sticky," they tend to cling to whatever instrument you scoop them out with.   This is especially true when they first hatch and are very small.

If the underbelly and legs are covered in maggots, I place the fawn in a bathtub lined with towels so the fawn doesn't slip or get cold, then hose the majority off using a handheld sprayer and warm water.   I thoroughly dry the fawn and put her on warmed bedding while I remove the remaining maggots.   It takes about three hours to remove them all and is back-breaking work.

In the past, we had no choice but to euthanize a fawn with maggots in the underbelly's subcutaneous tissue.   There was no way to remove them and the fawn's death would be slow and miserable.   However, in recent years, some rehabilitators have reported success using Capstar.   Although it's designed to rid a dog of a severe flea infestation (it kills fleas currently on the dog, not eggs or future fleas), some say it works on maggots, as well.   I have not tried this so I cannot say, but given the other options are either euthanasia or an agonizing death, I would say it's worth a try.

Prior to becoming a wildlife rehabilitator, I knew little about maggots (after all, what reason would I have to know?). I thought, as many do, that flies lay eggs on dead animals. However, flies seem to have a sixth sense when it comes to an animal in trouble and will lay eggs prior to the animal dying. When someone tells me flies are buzzing around an animal, I know without a single other question he's in trouble.

Eggs can be anywhere, or should I say everywhere - the fur, inside the ears, mouth or nose, the umbilicus, anus, you name it. For those new to rehabilitation and have never seen fly eggs, they are a "dirty" off-white color and look like tiny grains of rice. The eggs are in clumps and stuck on the animal with a type of adhesive, making them difficult to remove.

Having tried many removal methods, unfortunately the best way I've found is lengthy and back breaking. I take a dry washcloth or an old toothbrush (or both) and briskly rub where the eggs are. This breaks the "seal" and I can then comb the eggs out, or use my fingers to pick out the larger clumps.

Washing the fawn to get rid of eggs is not recommended. You end up with a wet deer covered in soggy fly eggs. Washing does not help remove the eggs, and given eggs hatch faster in the presence of moisture and heat... not a good idea.

Eggs can hatch quickly, in as little as an hour when it is hot and humid. Because maggots are much more difficult to eradicate than eggs, you should not delay removing them. Evidently you would deal with an active bleed or something life threatening first. Short of the obvious, however, do not put off dealing with the eggs simply because they don't seem that critical.

Meningeal worm

Most deer carry a number of meningeal worms without problem. However, if the numbers get too heavy, it can cause the deer to be uncoordinated, perhaps going in circles. Partial paralysis can also occur.

Nasal bots

Adult bot flies lay eggs around the deer's nose or mouth. Larvae then tunnel through the nasal passages. Once they develop, they leave the deer and pupate in the ground. Nasal bots are not considered problematic, even in large numbers, though my personal thought is having larvae wriggling around in your nasal passages must feel appalling.

Rodents

Food attracts mice, that's just a fact.   It's especially problematic for rehabbers who live in the country, and most who rehab deer do.   To keep mice at a minimum, keep foods (except those out for patients to eat) in metal containers with tight-fitting lids.

For mice that make their way indoors (and they seem to find the tiniest crack), you can use humane live traps to catch and release them outdoors where they belong.   Of all the traps I've used, I've had the best success with the Hav-A-Hart (name brand).   You need to check traps at least twice daily because mice die from stress if not released quickly.

Ticks

Ticks are found on most wild animals and deer are no exception.   In North America, 18 different species can live on deer, though some are more prevalent.

As with all animals, a few ticks create little problem.   They grab a ride, latch on, feed, then drop off once engorged.   However, heavy infestation can cause anemia, lethargy, and in severe cases, death.

Inflammation at the bite sites can become severe and lead to secondary bacterial infection. If infestation is massive, it can bring about blindness or death in younger fawns.   Ticks can be found on any part of the body, but tend to concentrate on the face, especially near the eyes and ears.

Because the tick that can carry Lyme disease is found on deer, there was once talk of wiping out deer to get rid of the tick.   Even though humans don't get Lyme disease directly from deer, many still felt it would be the way to go.   What they failed to consider was that same tick is found on other animals, including cats and dogs, squirrels, rabbits, raccoons, and birds, as well as how to carry out the mass murder plot!

VETERINARY ADVICE – TREATMENT PROTOCOLS

Dr. Chuck Miller of Triangle Veterinary Hospital in Durham, North Carolina (see About the Veterinarian on pg. 193) has been kind enough to lend his expertise to list medications appropriate for use in deer. It is a huge asset to this book. I received countless requests to give prescription and dosage information but since I am not a veterinarian, I could not legally or morally do so. With Dr. Miller's generosity, I can now include this.

If you have a deer that needs veterinarian assistance, take him to a vet in your area willing to work with wildlife. If he is unfamiliar with which medications to use for deer, you can present him with this chapter. Although I have intentionally avoided medical terminology, Dr. Miller is writing for another vet, so he is, naturally, going to use the correct and proper medical terminology.

Please note that all the information and wording in this section (except what I've written here or otherwise indicate) is from Dr. Miller. His treatment protocols may differ from mine since his are medicine based and mine are more natural based. However, none of his treatments conflict with mine (and vice versa).

Capture myopathy (Exertional rhabdomyolysis)

Unfortunately, once a deer sustains capture myopathy, the prognosis for survival is always grave. There is no treatment for capture myopathy, only supportive care, which is why prevention is critical.

The following supportive care can be attempted by your veterinarian:

1. IV fluids
   a. Lactated ringers solution at shock dose rate
   b. Monitor for response and correct rate as needed
   c. Diuresis is critical; monitor urine output
2. Antibiotics (if needed for injuries or infections)
   (see section on antibiotics - below)
3. Pain control (if needed)
   Critically important to decrease stress (see misc. medications- below)
4. Encourage eating & drinking as soon as possible
5. Consider humane euthanasia if condition does not improve or animal is suffering

Wound care

Prior to veterinarian treatment, general wound care principals should be followed.   Flush wounds at low pressure with clean warm water to remove debris, then cover wound with clean dressing.

Veterinary treatment:

- Clean wound with chlorhexadine (Novasan®) or dilute povidine iodine (Betadine®) solution
- Remove foreign material and devitalized tissue if required
- Surgical intervention may be indicated to treat injuries
- Antibiotic therapy as indicated (see section on antibiotics - below)
- Start pain medication as indicated (see misc. medications - below)

External parasite control

Ticks and maggots

- Remove manually
- Warm water flushes may facilitate maggot removal
- Fipronil spray (Frontline®) at 1 spray per pound is helpful for ticks

Lice

- Moxidextin (Cydectin®) pour on at 1 ml/10kg applied to hair along back whiskers to base of tail
- Ivermectin (Ivomec®) at 200 micrograms/kg sq

Ear mites

- Tresaderm ear drops at 2-3 drops to both ears twice daily for 7 days, stop 7 days and repeat for 7 days
- Ivermectin (Ivomec®) at above dose

Arterial worms (internal parasites)

Arterial worms *Elaephora schoneideri* are transmitted by horse flies. They reside in the carotid arteries and can cause food impactions with swelling in the intermandibular and ventral cervical areas.   Examine area to make sure they are not abscesses. Piperazine salts at 100 mg/lb by mouth have been used to treat this condition. Surgery may be indicated to drain the abscess if present and may be helpful in alleviating food impactions.

(Author's note: For more information on arterial worms, see "Parasites/Pest Control" on pg. 81.)

Transport sedation

- Sedation may not be needed if the deer is calm and a dark transport box is utilized.
- Diazepan (Valium) at 2-5 mg IV (total dose) provides excellent sedation that usually lasts for 30 - 45 min.

Anesthesia

Preoperative

- Adults - withhold food and water for 12 hours
- Infants - withhold food and water for 2 - 4 hours

Pre-medication

- Meditomidine (Dormitor®)   .05 mg/kg IM or IV (can reverse effects with Antipamezole (Antesedan)   .25 mg/kg IM)
- Butorphanol   2 mg/kg IV

Induction

- Mask induction with Isoflurane or Sevoflurane can be used in calm small deer
- Ketamine   2 mg/kg IV following premedication

Maintenance

- Isoflurane or Sevoflurane via endotracheal tube (ET tube)
- Post operative
- Leave ET tube in place until laryngeal reflex returns
- Lower head to allow drainage of saliva
- Position deer on right side or sternal recumbency post intubation

Antibiotics safe for white-tailed deer

- Ceftiofur (Naxcell®)   dosage: 1.1 - 2.2 mg/kg IM qd x 3 treatments or as needed
- Penicillin G procaine   dosage: 40,000 - 66,000 IU/kg IM or SQ qd as needed
- Enrofloxacin   (Baytril®)   dosage: 10 mg/kg PO qd as needed
- Oxytetracycline long acting (Liquamycin LA 200®)   dosage: 10 - 20 mg/kg IM qd 24 - 48 hours as needed (may be useful in decreasing the incidence or preinatal infections)

Miscellaneous medications

- Butorphanol   dosage: .1 - .4 mg/kg IV or IM as needed for pain control

NATURE'S MEDICINE CABINET

<u>Overview</u>

At our wildlife facility, we have used herbs, supplements, homeopathy, and natural healing methods from the beginning. I have utilized these modalities for well over two decades on myself, family, pets, and the wildlife. They work gently but effectively and if used properly, can work wonders. I have seen amazing recoveries from natural medicines. In addition, herbs are inexpensive compared to traditional meds. They are easy to find and do not require a prescription.

In spite of their wide margin of safety, it is important to understand herbs are still medicine and should be used with care. Just because a product is available over the counter does not mean it can be used casually. Anything, and that includes water, can prove dangerous or fatal if taken incorrectly. By the same token, unbelievably high numbers of people have serious reactions (including death) to prescription medications, yet you rarely hear about that. Serious reactions to herbs are rare, but one should still use caution and common sense.

Not everyone believes in herbs and natural healing. Some think of it as voo-doo or something backwoods folk who can't afford "real" medicine use. Some veterinarians scoff at the use of herbs, whereas others are totally open to their use. Others believe in relying primarily on traditional medicine, using herbs for more minor problems. The important thing is to find a vet whose belief system best matches your own. That is not saying you will always agree with each other, but you should have the same general belief system. If you are a big believer in natural methods, you don't want a vet who thinks they are ridiculous. If you are a firm believer in traditional medicine and your veterinarian believes mostly in natural methods, that would not be a good match either. This is especially true when choosing a vet for your pets, but also when working with a veterinarian with the wildlife.

(*Personal anecdote: my very first vet (now retired) was a man I adored in spite of the fact he never gave any credence to the herbs. Regardless of how many successes we had, he always chalked it up to coincidence. Our first rescued/adopted dog survived distemper, but it left scar tissue on his brain. As a result, he suffered frequent grand mal seizures for which he was put on strong drugs. We were told the medicine would damage his liver and shorten his life, but that we had no alternative. Even on the highest dose allowable, he would still have seizures about every 6 weeks, as many as a dozen over a 24 hour period. After ten years of this, I started him on herbs and supplements. I had gotten into natural healing for myself by this time and figured it might work for my pets, too. He went from a dozen seizures in a 24 hour period every six weeks to a single seizure annually... a dramatic difference!*

Another rescued dog not only tested positive for heartworms, but was symptomatic.   I was told without immediate treatment he would soon die and it would be very painful. However, I had concerns about the traditional toxic method of dealing with heartworms so, to my vet's chagrin, I opted to treat with herbs instead.   Not only did it rid my dog of heartworms, he lived another 15 years.

Another rescue developed a very aggressive form of cancer when he was 15.   My vet hugged me as he broke the news that my dog had just two months to live.   Two additional vets confirmed it was this aggressive cancer.   I immediately started my dog on four herbs. I could not see the internal tumors, of course, but the external ones were quite visible.   I thought they were getting smaller, but my family thought it was just false hope.   It took time, but the tumors disappeared.   After a year of no tumors, we took him off herbs, assuming they were no longer necessary.   The tumors returned with a vengeance so back on the herbs he went.   Instead of two months, he lived three years, dying at the ripe old age of 18 or 19.   (Since all our dogs are rescues, we don't know their exact age so we approximate, then choose a birthday from that). I have had a couple vets since tell me the original diagnosis must have been wrong, there is no way my dog could have lived three years with that type of cancer.   They would prefer to believe three vets got it wrong than accept that the herbs worked.   Anyway, these are just a couple examples of the amazing results we've had with herbs.   This is not to say you would have the same results I did with these illnesses, but I have had too many successes to chalk it up to coincidence.)

With the advent of the internet, it is easy to research herbs, supplements, etc.   One should visit numerous websites to learn about a natural medicine, as well as read lots of books. You should not rely on one source, nor should you use an herb because your best friend's cousin's sister's neighbor swears by it.   Consult several reliable sources to discover the general consensus.   Learn which herbs should not be mixed with which traditional medicines.   Some herbs are considered unsafe by the FDA.   Whether they actually are, I steer clear since there are plenty of other herbs for the same ailment, so why take unnecessary chances?

Reference books

Two books I use quite often are: <u>Prescription for Nutritional Healing</u> by James Balch and <u>Natural Health for Dogs and Cats</u> by Richard Pitcairn.   The first is written for people, but much of the information works for non-humans.   The second book is written for animals, though not specifically wildlife.   Balch's book recommends herbs and supplements most often, whereas Pitcairn advocates homeopathy more.   There are many good books available on natural healing.   These are simply the two I find myself referring to most often.   Another book I recommend is the Physicians' Desk Reference for Herbal Medicines.   Doctors have a book called the Physicians' Desk Reference (PDR) that they utilize for information on prescription (and over-the-counter) medicines.   A few years ago, they came out with a PDR for herbs.   Since so many people are self-treating, doctors realized they could not just dismiss herbs.   At the same time, they were uncomfortable okaying them or prescribing medications to use alongside when they knew little about herbal medicine.   The PDR for Herbs lets doctors know which herbs are considered safe, if a particular herb doesn't mix well with certain prescription medicines, etc.   Although the book is written for doctors, it is a good resource for us, as well.

Purchasing herbs

It is important to purchase herbs from a reliable source.   Because there are so few laws governing the sale of herbs, you could easily receive inferior product and not know it.   I buy my herbs from either Penn Herb Company or the Vitamin Shoppe (see Supplies & Where to Find Them on pg. 17)

Something else to keep in mind, by law herbs are sold as food or dietary supplements, not medicine.   Therefore, directions will say "As a dietary supplement, take one - three capsules three times daily."   You can look at dozens of products and the information will be almost word for word.   So to find the proper dosage, you have to research, not rely on the bottle's label.   I find this disconcerting.   However, the herb and supplement manufacturers are simply following the rules as they currently exist.

Except where noted, herbs should be purchased in capsule (powder) form vs. tinctures or other versions.   Not only do herbs work better in that form (for these uses), it allows you to open the capsule, sprinkle out the amount you need, then close the capsule to keep it fresh until needed again.

Note: Penn Herb's capsules are twice the size of a regular capsule.   I have taken that into account in the dosage information for any of Penn's proprietary blends.   However, single herbs are dosed for a regular size capsule.   If you purchase your individual herbs from Penn, you should cut the dosage in half since theirs are twice the size.

List of herbs

These are just some of the herbs/supplements/natural medicines I use. Some I utilize rarely, others I rely on all the time. (There are many other herbs I highly recommend, just not for deer, so they are not listed here).

Next to each herb, I give the scientific name, common names it is known by, and the disorders I recommend them for. Most herbs have many more applications than what I list. For example, I might list an herb as being useful for respiratory problems. That herb might also be beneficial for stomach issues, but I don't mention that since there are other herbs that work better for the stomach. If I listed every potential use for every single herb, it would not only be extremely lengthy, but confusing.

A nice thing about herbs is you do not have to be exact with dosing. Some are more potent than others, but unless you seriously misuse them, they are very safe. I am including a general guideline of how much to use for a fawn up to 20 pounds. Increase accordingly for larger deer.

There are many more herbs available than what I've cited. Believe it or not, this is just a fraction. Where appropriate, I mention what part of the plant you are looking for. This is especially important with herbs where different parts are used for different things. The leaves of one plant might be beneficial for a certain ailment, while the roots might be good for a different illness altogether. The herbs I use frequently are marked with an *.

* __alfalfa__ - *"Medicago sativa"*

(also known as buffalo herb, purple medic)

A general restorative for an animal recovering from illness or injury. It has other uses, including building the blood, helping joints, and soothing the intestines.

<u>Dosage</u>: 1/4 capsule 1-3 times daily

* <u>aloe vera (juice)</u>

Used externally for burns, internally for gastroenteritis. Purchase 100% pure aloe juice designed to be taken internally. Juice for internal consumption can be used externally but gel meant for external use is not necessarily safe for ingesting.

<u>Dosage</u>: external- as needed/internal- .5 cc 1 - 3 times daily up to 3 days

<u>anise (seed)</u> - *"Pimpinella anisum"*

Good for digestion; alleviates gas, bloating, or colic; helps relieve nausea.

<u>Dosage</u>: 1/8 capsule every 2-4 hours as needed

<u>angelica</u> - see dong quai

* <u>Antispasmodic Mixture</u>

A proprietary herbal blend by Penn Herb useful for all types of circumstances where spasms are a problem, such as muscle cramps, stomach cramps (e.g. colic), spasms of the bladder, and so on. This blend also has a calming effect on the nervous system.

<u>Dosage</u>: 1/8 capsule every 4-6 hours as needed

* <u>arnica</u> - *"Arnica montana"*

The homeopathic form is excellent for patients who are injured and bruised. The tablet is placed under the tongue (sublingual). Arnica also comes in a spray for external use to help prevent bruising and soreness. Arnica spray should not be used in the eyes, mouth or other delicate areas.

<u>Dosage</u>: external- spray on affected area just once/internal- see dispenser for dosage information and use 1/4 amount recommended.

<u>Note</u>: arnica, the herb, should not be used internally. It is poisonous. It is only safe to use internally in the homeopathic form!

basil - *"Ocinum basilicum"*

Externally this herb can help draw toxins from stings and bites.   It can also be made into a tea to externally treat fungal skin infections, ringworm, or thrush.   Internal use treats indigestion, gas, or nausea.

Dosage: external- as needed/internal- 1/8 capsule every 6 hours as needed.

bistort (root) - *"Polygonum bistorta"*

(also known as patience dock, sweet dock, Easter giant, dragonwort)

Treats diarrhea and digestive disorders.   Also used (internally) for external and internal bleeding.

Dosage: for GI issues 1/8 capsule every 4 hours as needed.   For bleeding, 1/8 capsule.   Give second dose in 30 minutes - one hour if bleeding has not stopped.   If bleeding still does not stop, switch to a different herb.

blackberry (leaves) - *"Rubus villosus"*

Treats diarrhea.   Also helps with colds and sore throats.

Dosage: 1/8 - 1/4 capsule 1-3 times/day as needed.

* black tea wash

Boil regular black tea bag in a small amount of water to make a strong tea.   Cool.   Either dab with gauze or drizzle on the area with a syringe.   Black tea is a gentle, but effective, way to clean wounds and the tannins help the wounds heal.

Dosage: externally as needed

* <u>**blueberry (leaves)**</u> - *"Vaccinium myrtillus"*

(also known as bilberry, huckleberry, whortleberry)

Useful for eye problems; helps strengthen the eyes.

<u>Dosage</u>: 1/8 capsule twice daily.

<u>**buchu (leaves)**</u> - *"Barosma crenata"*

Natural diuretic.   Helps promote the flow of urine.   Calms the bladder.

<u>Dosage</u>: 1/8 capsule 1-3 times/day up to three days.

<u>**butcher's broom**</u> - *"Ruscus aculeatus"*

(also known as knee holly, kneeholm, sweet broom)

For head trauma, either instead of, or in addition to, gingko biloba.

<u>Dosage</u>: 1/8 capsule 2-3 times/day.

<u>**calendula (tea or gel)**</u> - *"Calendula officinalis"*

(also known as marigold)

Very healing to irritated or chafed skin.   Heals minor wounds and abrasions.

<u>Dosage</u>: external as needed

<u>Note</u>: Do not use on deep wounds.   Do not use on delicate areas, such as genitals, around eyes, etc.

* <u>cascara sagrada (bark)</u> - *"Rhamnus purshiana"*

*(*also known as chittem bark, sacred bark)

Good for constipation.

<u>Dosage</u>: 1/8 capsule 1-2 times/day as needed.

<u>Note</u>:   Be sure you are treating constipation and not an impaction.

<u>catnip</u> - *"Nepeta cataria"*

(also known as catmint)

Given this herb tends to turn kitties a bit wacky, it is surprising to learn it actually calms other species down.   Also relieves gas or bloating.

<u>Dosage</u>: 1/8 capsule every 4 hours as needed.

* <u>cayenne (pepper)</u> - *"Capsicum annuum"*

(also known as African bird pepper, capsicum)

Old remedy for internal bleeding.   I have used it many, many times.   It works extremely well.   Put a small amount in white grape or apple juice to make it more palatable.   Helps with circulation.

<u>Dosage</u>: 1/8 capsule (or less). Can give second dose in 30 minutes - one hour if needed.

* <u>chamomile, German</u> - *"Matricaria chamomilla"*

Relieves gas and bloating.   Helps relax the digestive tract.   Good for calming muscle spasms and cramps.   Soothes the nervous system.   Very gentle, extremely safe.

<u>Dosage</u>: 1/8 - 1/4 capsule every 3-4 hours as needed.

charcoal, willow - *"Salix alba"*

(also known as wood charcoal)

Most rehabbers are familiar with activated charcoal, which is basically a concentrated form of willow charcoal.   Can be used for acid indigestion, gas, bloating, nausea, vomiting, or diarrhea.   Charcoal absorbs toxins, which is why activated charcoal is often used in oral poisonings.   Because charcoal does work by absorption, it should only be used occasionally as it will also absorb nutrients your body needs.

Dosage: 1/4 capsule every 4 hours up to two doses.

* coltsfoot (leaves) - *"Tussilago farfara"*

(also known as bullsfoot, British tobacco, coughwort, foal's foot, horsehoof)

Very soothing to the throat and respiratory system.

Dosage: 1/8 capsule 2-3 times daily

cornflower - *"Centaurea cyanus"*

(also known as cyani, bachelor's button or bluebottle)

Taken orally, it provides relief from stings and bites.   Also an old native American remedy for venomous snake and spider bites.   Wild animals can get bitten or stung just like humans and pets.   Like people, they can also sometimes have allergic (anaphylactic) reactions, as well, in which case they would need antihistamine and emergency vet care.

Dosage: 1/8 - 1/4 capsule.

cornsilk - *"Zea mays"*

(also known as Indian corn, maize, maize silk, mother's hair)

Mild, but effective, diuretic.

Dosage: 1/8 capsule every 4-6 hours as needed up to 3 days.

cramp bark - *"Viburnum opulus"*

(also known as high cranberry, rose elder, squaw bush, whitten tree)

As the name implies, it is good for muscle spasm.

Dosage: 1/8 capsule every 6 hours as needed.

dong quai - *"Angelica sinensis"*

(also known as Chinese angelica)

For when the body is bruised and sore after an accident.

Dosage: 1/8 capsule twice daily.

echinacea (root) - *"Echinacea angustifolia"*

(also known as American coneflower, black sampson, purple coneflower)

Helps build the immune system.   If an animal gets sick, it can be given to his pen mates to, hopefully, keep them from getting sick, too (or at least not as severely).

Dosage: 1/8 capsule 3 times daily up to 10 days (no longer).

* eyebright - *"Euphrasia officinalis"*

Excellent for eye ailments.   Can be taken internally, as well as made into a dilute tea and used in the eyes as a rinse.

Dosage: external - as needed/internal - 1/8 capsule daily

* Eyebright Formula

A proprietary blend by Penn Herb for eye infections or eye problems. Use internally only. Unlike plain eyebright, this blend contains other herbs so it cannot be made into a tea for direct use in the eyes.

Dosage: 1/8 capsule 1-2 times daily.

fennel (seed) - *"Foenicum vulgare"*

(also known as large fennel, Roman fennel)

Excellent for bloat, gas or colic. Fennel can act as a suppressant to the appetite, so if you have an underweight or emaciated patient, choose a different herb.

Dosage: 1/8 capsule (or less) every 6 hours as needed.

* garlic oil - *"Allium sativum"*

Use on infected wounds. Garlic is a natural antibiotic, antifungal and antiviral. Due to an oil base, it will work its way into the "nooks and crannies." Unlike ointment, it will not seal the wound, allowing it instead to breathe and heal.

Dosage: externally - as needed

Note: garlic oil is garlic in an olive oil base. It can be used on even deep wounds. It does not sting, but does have a strong smell. In addition to clearing up infection (or keeping infection from setting in), it keeps flies away from wounds.

ginger (root) - "Zingiber officinale"

Most widely used with digestive problems such as upset stomach, indigestion or nausea. Helps with circulation so it would be useful for a deer that cannot be up and about.

Dosage: 1/8 capsule every 6 hours as needed.

* __gingko biloba (leaves)__   - *"gingko biloba"*

(also known as fossil tree, maidenhair tree)

For patients with head trauma.

Dosage: 1/8 capsule 1-2 times daily.

Note: Gingko does thin the blood so it should not be used in conjunction with aspirin or on an animal you know (or suspect) is bleeding internally or externally.

* __hawthorn (berries)__ - *"Crateagus oxycantha"*

(also known as common hawthorn, English hawthorn, May tree, thorn apple tree, whitehorn)

Works great for any type heart problem.   Rather than raising or lowering the blood pressure as some herbs do, hawthorn berries regulate the heart.   If it is beating too weakly and slowly, it will help it beat stronger.   If beating too hard and fast, it will help it beat slower and more regular.

Dosage: 1/8 capsule 1-2 times daily.

* __horsetail__ - *"Equisetum arvense"*

(also known as bottle brush, pewterwort, scouring rush, shave grass)

Works for internal bleeding.   It's also a diuretic.   But what it does best is heal broken bones. It works so well you should not begin using until the break has been set.   Otherwise it could start mending in the wrong position.

Dosage: 1/8 capsule twice daily

Note: Do not use on an animal that has cardiac or renal problems.

hydrangea (root) - *"Hydrangea arborescens"*

(also known as wild hydrangea, seven barks)

Good for spinal injuries.   Acts much like cortisone, but without the potential problems or the need to slowly wean off of it.

Dosage: 1/16 capsule twice daily for up to three days.

* Kid's Ear Clear Oil

A proprietary blend of oils by Penn Herb for ear issues, including earaches, ear mites, and infection.

Dosage: per instructions on bottle

* lady's slipper - *"Cypripedium pubescens"*

(also known as nerve root, moccasin flower, American valerian, nerveroot, whippoorwill's-shoe, yellow Indian shoe)

Useful for pain, but also works well for patients that are stressed and upset.   It has a mild sedative effect.

Dosage: 1/8 capsule every 4 - 6 hours as needed.

* licorice (root) - *"Glycyrrhiza glabra"*

(also known as sweet root)

Excellent for sore throats and respiratory issues.   Also works great as a diuretic - mild but effective (I have often used in lieu of lasix).

Dosage: 1/8 capsule every 4 hours.

Note: licorice root does raise the blood pressure, so do not use with deer where that could be a problem.

* <u>lobelia</u> - *"Lobelia inflata"*

(also known as asthma weed, emetic herb, Indian tobacco)

Good for any type spasmodic pain.   Is also sedating.

<u>Dosage:</u> 1/8 capsule every 6 hours as needed.

<u>marshmallow (leaves)</u> - *"Althaea officinalis"*

(also known as althea, sweet weed)

Good for pneumonia or lung ailments, helps quiet a cough (especially a dry one)

<u>Dosage:</u> 1/8 capsule 3 times daily.

<u>meadowsweet</u> - *"Spiraea ulmaria"*

(also known as queen of the meadow herb (not to be confused with queen of the meadow <u>root</u>)

Excellent for muscle spasm, whether from an accident or illness.

<u>Dosage:</u> 1/8 capsule every 4-6 hours.

* <u>milk thistle</u> - *"Silybum marianum"*

(also known as marian thistle, Mary thistle, Our Lady's thistle)

For treating any type of liver problem or damage, regardless of cause.

<u>Dosage:</u> 1/8 capsule 2-3 times daily.

oregon grape (root) - *"Berberis aquifolium"*

(also known as California barberry, holly-leaved barberry, mountain grape)

Works well with skin issues, allowing toxins to exit the body.   In deer, it is useful for dermatophilosis.

<u>Dosage</u>: 1/8 capsule daily.

* pau d' arco (bark) - *"Tabebuia avellanedae"*

(also known as taheebo)

Fantastic for treating infection, as well as cancers and tumors.   It can be beneficial for deer with cutaneous fibromas.

<u>Dosage</u>: 1/8 capsule once or twice daily.

peppermint (leaves) - *"Mentha piperita"*

Very soothing for upset stomachs, but also useful for animals in shock or bordering on shock.

<u>Dosage</u>: 1/8 capsule (or less) every 2-4 hours as needed.

* probiotics

Animals (human and non-human) have good bacteria in their digestive tracts.   The good bacteria help our GI tracts function properly, much like a septic system relies on bacteria to work.   Antibiotics cannot discriminate between good and bad bacteria; they destroy them all. If good bacteria are not added back, not only does the GI tract become out of whack, it leaves a vacancy for bad bacteria to move in.   Probiotics are a wide assortment of good bacteria. My preferred choice are those that come in a small, round, hard-cased "bead" (sometimes referred to as a pearl).   Not only are they easy to swallow, but the casing remains intact until the bead reaches the ideal area for the probiotics to be released.

It may be difficult, however, to get a fawn to swallow the beads, even as small as they are. For that reason, I recommend a powdered probiotic instead.   You can use whatever brand you prefer, just be sure it is a good one.   I like Ultimate 10 Probiotics (see Supplies & Where to Find Them - pg. 21)

* Rescue Remedy

A homeopathic tincture for a patient in shock or stressed.   Especially useful when a patient first comes in.

Dosage: follow directions on bottle.

* Respiratory Defense

This is a proprietary blend by Penn Herb (see Supplies & Where to Find Them - pg. 21).   For patients with any kind of respiratory ailment.

Dosage: 1/8 capsule 3 times daily.

schizandra (berry) - *"Schisandra chinensis"*

Good for promoting energy; supports the immune system; heals the liver; good for kidney health; strengthens the respiratory system.   Basically a good overall tonic for an animal on the mend.

Dosage: 1/8 capsule twice daily as needed.

shepherd's purse - *"Capsella bursa pastoris"*

(also known as lady's purse, mother's heart, St. James' weed)

Used primarily to stop bleeding.   It works by constricting blood vessels, so it should not be used with a patient where that could be detrimental.

Dosage: 1/8 capsule (or less).   May give another dose in 30 minutes - one hour if needed.

106

* <u>slippery elm (bark)</u> - *"Ulmus fulva"*

(also known as elm, Indian elm, moose elm, red elm)

You know the old "if I were stranded on a deserted island" scenario?   Well, this is one herb I would choose if shipwrecked and could only have ten herbs with me.   Slippery elm is good for anything GI related.   Great for diarrhea, gas, colic, problems digesting milk, gastroenteritis, as well as serious GI illness, like e. coli or salmonella.

Put the appropriate amount in the animal's bottle, in juice, applesauce or whatever.   It becomes gelatinous, so it should be used quickly.

<u>Dosage</u>: 1/8 - 1/4 capsule every 4 - 6 hours as needed.

<u>spearmint</u> - *"Mentha spicata"*

For all types of digestive problems, including upset stomach, nausea, vomiting, and gas.   Has a mild sedative effect, calming frazzled nerves.   It's also a mild diuretic, good for urinary tract problems.

<u>Dosage</u>: 1/8 capsule every 4-6 hours as needed.

* <u>uva ursi</u> - *"Arctostaphylos uva ursi"*

(also known as barberry, bearberry, mountain cranberry, upland cranberry)

Excellent for anything urinary tract related.

<u>Dosage</u>: 1/8 capsule daily for up to 2-3 days.   (Can take longer, just typically don't need to.)

<u>vervain</u> - *"Verbena officinalis"*

(also known as blue vervain, verbena)

Good for relaxing and calming a distressed patient.

<u>Dosage</u>: 1/8 capsule every 4 hours as needed.

* <u>vitamin C</u>

Use to reduce swelling with head trauma and/or back injury, as well as general healing. An excessive amount of vitamin C can loosen the stool, but it is water soluble and does not build up in the body. Excess amounts are excreted through the urine.

<u>Dosage</u>: 250 mg. every 4-8 hours for 2-3 days.

* <u>vitamin E oil</u>

Excellent for wounds that are not infected. Helps them heal quickly with minimal or no scarring.

<u>Dosage</u>: external - as needed.

<u>white willow (bark)</u> - *"Salix alba"*

(also known as salacin willow)

For mild pain. White willow bark contains natural ingredients that were later synthesized to create aspirin.

<u>Dosage</u>: 1/8 - 1/4 capsule every 4 hours as needed.

Treating the ailments naturally

The previous section lists herbs and supplements alphabetically and in detail. However, I am also listing various ailments and injuries, then which natural products you can use. Otherwise you would have to read through each herb/supplement to find the ailment. Hopefully this will allow you to find what you need in a more timely fashion. The remedies I prefer are marked with an *.

bites/stings	basil * cornflower
bleeding	bistort * cayenne horsetail shepherd's purse
broken bones	* horsetail
bruising/soreness	* arnica dong quai meadowsweet
burns	* aloe vera gel
constipation	* cascara sagrada
cough	marshmallow
circulation	* cayenne ginger
diarrhea	bistort root blackberry charcoal, willow * kaolin pectin
diuretic	buchu cornsilk horsetail * licorice spearmint
ear issues	* Kid's Ear Clear Oil * garlic oil
eye infection/problems	blueberry * eyebright * Eyebright Formula
general health/restorative	* alfalfa schizandra vitamin C

head trauma	butcher's broom * gingko biloba * vitamin C
heart problems	* hawthorn berries
immune system (builds)	* alfalfa echinacea
liver issues	* milk thistle schizandra
pain: general	* lady's slipper white willow bark
pain: spasm	* Antispasmodic Mixture chamomile, German cramp bark * lobelia meadowsweet
poison/toxins	charcoal, willow * cornflower
respiratory issues	coltsfoot licorice marshmallow * Respiratory Defense schizandra
sedative/stress	catnip chamomile * lady's slipper * lobelia Rescue Remedy spearmint vervain
shock	peppermint * Rescue Remedy
sore throat	blackberry coltsfoot licorice * marshmallow vitamin C
skin issues	aloe vera gel NOTE: my preference basil depends on skin disorder calendula ointment oregon grape
spinal injury	Antispasdomic Mixture dong quai * hydrangea meadowsweet * vitamin C

stomach issues: gas, colic, bloating	anise Antispasmodic Mixture basil bistort root catnip chamomile, German * fennel ginger probiotics * slippery elm spearmint
stomach issues: gastroenteritis	aloe vera juice charcoal, willow probiotics * slippery elm
stomach issues: nausea &/or vomiting	anise basil charcoal, willow * ginger * peppermint slippery elm
urinary tract/kidney/bladder issues	schizandra spearmint * uva ursi buchu
wound care: cleaning the wound	* black tea rinse
wound care: treating the uninfected wound	* vitamin E oil * aloe vera gel calendula ointment vitamin C (internal) alfalfa (internal)
wound care: treating the infected area	* garlic oil

WHEN A DEER CANNOT BE SAVED: EUTHANASIA OPTIONS

It is always heartbreaking when any animal in our care cannot be saved, but it is a sad reality.   Sometimes the animal dies on his own, other times he needs to be euthanized. The judgment to euthanize is left up to the rehabilitator (except in states that have regulations governing such decisions.)   If a deer is savable but not releasable, some states will issue permanent captive permits, others will not.

Euthanasia can be performed by a veterinarian using drugs.   That isn't always feasible, however.   The deer may be out in the boonies along a deserted road, it might be a holiday or late at night.   There are many times getting an injured deer (particularly an adult) to a vet or getting a vet to the deer is improbable.   In those cases, euthanasia by gunshot, done properly, is humane, albeit admittedly unpleasant for the person doing it and those witnessing it.   It may seem barbaric, but the brain stem is severed resulting in an instant brain death.

Although there are people who will grab a rifle or shotgun to "put an animal down," a 22 or 38 pistol is safer and easier to handle, as well as control.   A rifle or shotgun is, literally, overkill and there is a risk of the bullet going through the animal and ricocheting.

There are those taught to shoot an animal "right between the eyes," but the skull can veer the bullet off its intended course.   Instead, most wildlife officials recommend placing the pistol at the back of the head.   You can feel an indention between the base of the skull and the top of the vertebrae.   Position the pistol at that area, 1 - 3 inches away.   Aim slightly upward so the resulting gunshot will sever the brain stem.   Be aware: instant brain death is not instant body death.   It will take a few minutes for the body to shut down so you may see breathing, jerking, or other movement after the shot.   It can be disconcerting, especially if people don't understand the deer isn't feeling anything.

(Author's note: For me, I find it less upsetting if the deer is sedated ahead of time.   I know it isn't necessary, or always practical, but it makes it easier.   Not easy, mind you, but easier. It may also be less traumatic (depending on the person) if the head and face of the deer are covered and you don't have to look them in the eye.   If so, use a lightweight sheet or blanket, then feel with a finger for proper placement of the pistol.   Just be sure, of course, to move your hand out of the way before firing the weapon!)

At times you will get calls about an adult deer hit by a car that cannot get up.   After asking lots of questions (see Injured Adult Deer section on pg. 118), if you determine it is not something anyone can fix, suggest the caller contact their area law enforcement (sheriff or police) to have the deer euthanized (sometimes referred to by law enforcement as "dispatched").

(Author's note: Once law enforcement and I both responded to a call about a badly injured deer. To avoid insulting them, I never shared the proper way to shoot a deer. The deputy ended up having to shoot the doe four times before she finally died. He was in tears, I was crying, the public was outraged. From then on, I tell law enforcement "you probably already know this, but..." then explain how we do it. That way, if they did actually know, I have prefaced it so as to not question their abilities. If they did not know, they did now. If they want to say "I already knew that" when, in reality, they didn't, it doesn't matter as long as the deer doesn't suffer and the officer wasn't made to look ignorant.)

Disposal of a deer body

If a deer is euthanized with medication or has a contagious disease, disposing of the body becomes a safety issue. Be sure to bury the deer deep enough that dogs, foxes, or other animals cannot dig the body up, and place large rocks on top the grave.

If the deer does not have toxic medicines in his system and there is no contagious illness to worry about, disposal can be one of several methods: burial; disposal in the landfill (animal carcass area); or placement on your property where wildlife (such as opossums, vultures, etc.) can use the body for food and any decayed material will fertilize the soil. You will want to put it far enough from your residence that the smell of decay does not reach you. Avoid placing the body near a body of water or on someone else's property. Check your area's regulations before choosing a disposal method to be certain you aren't breaking any rules.

HANDLING DEER CALLS FROM THE PUBLIC

Orphaned vs. kidnapped - helping the "abandoned" fawn

When a doe gives birth, usually to two fawns, she does not stay with them the first couple weeks of their lives. She places them in (what she considers) good hiding places, typically putting each in a different location so if a predator comes across one, he won't necessarily find the other.

It is while these little guys are lying alone that people sometimes stumble across them and think they have been abandoned. Sometimes the fawn genuinely needs assistance, but usually not. In order to help the person determine if the fawn needs help, a rehabilitator should ask:

- Is the fawn quiet or crying? Although sometimes a fawn is silent because he is too weak to cry, normally a quiet fawn is a good sign. One crying incessantly does need help. No doe would allow her baby to bleat like that and not check on him.   Since a crying animal may as well have a neon sign pointing out his location to predators, babies know not to call out unless there is a serious problem.

- Are flies around the fawn? If so, the fawn needs help. We all have flies irritate us now and again when we are outdoors, but numerous flies, particularly the noisy green ones, buzzing around a fawn is a bad sign. (see External Parasites – Flies on pg. 82)

- Do you see any sign of diarrhea (such as anal staining), blood, broken bones, etc? Any of these means the fawn needs assistance.

- How is the fawn positioned? If the fawn is sitting in a normal position for a deer or lying sternally with his head down, that is a good sign. Lying on his side, particularly if he doesn't sit up when you reach him, could indicate a problem.

- Did a dog drag or chase the fawn? If the fawn was brought up by a dog, then he needs medical intervention.   If the fawn was chased, but not caught, the fawn may need assistance.   If you have no idea where the chase originated, then you have no clue where to return the little one to reunite with his mother.   Depending on the length of the pursuit, how hot it is, etc., chances are the fawn will need treatment for capture myopathy (see Injuries - capture myopathy - pg. 68).   If the person was walking their dog, saw the pursuit begin, the dog did not get hold of the fawn and they were able to stop the dog quickly, you can advise them to

115

confine their pet, then return the fawn to where he was before the chase began. However, the answer to all of the above must be yes, not just some. Otherwise the fawn will need intervention. For example, if the person saw the chase begin, the dog did not get hold of the fawn, but it took a while to stop the pursuit, then the little deer will need assistance. If the person saw the chase start, stopped it rapidly, but the dog got hold of the fawn, you will need to provide care.

Asking if the fawn looks thin is not a good way to determine if he needs help because all fawns look like beanpoles! Only someone who regularly deals with fawns can tell, by looking, if one is underweight or just naturally skinny. Therefore, I would not include this question. If the caller mentions it, I would not ignore their observation, but if everything else indicates the fawn is okay, I would not intervene based on that "factor" alone.

So the bottom line is if the fawn is very small; sitting quietly in a grassy or wooded area; has no flies, blood, diarrhea, or obvious injuries; and looks healthy and happy in spite of being alone, he should be left just that...alone!

If the fawn does not need assistance and the person has not moved him, advise them to leave him alone. If the fawn did not need intervention but has already been taken, have the caller put the fawn back if not too much time has gone by. The faster they are returned, the better. As closely as possible, the fawn needs to be put back in the same spot he was found. How much time is too much is open for debate. My recommendation is preferably less than 12. Certainly if the person has had the fawn for days or weeks, it is too late to reunite him with his mother. In that case, educate the caller so he does not make the mistake again.

If the fawn is returned to the area his mother left him, the caller can check on him in six hours. If the site is remote, the caller can take another person along for safety reasons, but it should not be a group affair. Inform the person they should not sit and watch for mom as she can detect the caller much sooner than he can detect the doe. She will not go to her baby as long as she knows someone is there. In six hours, if the fawn is still there, quiet and peaceful, leave him alone and again leave the area. The mother does not always move a fawn to another site between nursings, particularly if it appears to her to be a good hiding place.

If the fawn is gone, fine. The caller should not search for him, although it is okay to stand there a few minutes to listen for crying. A quiet fawn is a good sign. One incessantly hollering for his mother is not. If, at the second check the situation has changed (i.e. worsened), the caller should get the fawn to a licensed rehabilitator immediately.

As with any species, tell the caller not to give the fawn milk. Keep him warm and quiet, in subdued lighting, away from dogs and humans. Tell the person to keep their children, neighbors, and friends away from the fawn.   No posing with the fawn for pictures, no petting him, etc.   If it will be a while before they can get the fawn to you, they can give rehydrating fluids with an eyedropper or syringe if you (the rehabilitator) thinks he needs something.

If an injured fawn is found, tell them to not chase him. If they cannot quickly and easily get the fawn wrapped in a sheet and put in a pen or carrier, as hard as it is to do, they should leave him alone. Extensive chasing can kill him.   If he can run, he at least has a chance to survive. They may later find the fawn in a more weakened condition where they can then easily capture him.

If they put the fawn in a dog lot or similar area and he "goes crazy" trying to get out (e.g. banging into the walls), they should release him unless someone is in a position to tranquilize him. Otherwise, he may break his neck, severely damage his mouth and jaw, break a leg, or die from stress.   It is not an easy decision to release a fawn that should still be nursing, but if he is big and well enough to fight that hard, he has a better chance released than banging repeatedly into a fence.

If a fawn is injured

Sometimes, with enough questions, you can ascertain the fawn is untreatable, especially after you have been doing this a while.   A fawn with three legs severed by farming equipment is never going to be releasable, even if he lives.   If a fawn has intestines strewn all over the road, both eyes missing...anything blatant like this, it is perfectly reasonable to tell the caller the fawn needs to be euthanized and advise them to contact their veterinarian.

Some may balk believing that is "your job."   However, I learned the hard way over the years, we cannot do and be everything to everyone.   We should, by no means, pawn off our responsibilities on others, but there are things the public can handle with guidance from us, whether rigging a nest for baby birds when the old one has been destroyed or taking an animal to the vet for euthanasia when it is apparent nothing else can be done.

Obviously if you aren't certain, you should examine the fawn, but in a case where there is no doubt, there is no reason for you to drive to pick up the fawn only to turn right around and drive him to a vet for euthanasia.   Not to mention the additional stress on the fawn and added time he would suffer.   The public may complain, but it is not unreasonable or unfair to ask them to handle it.

The caller may question if they will be charged. That is up to the vet. Hopefully, if it is one they use for their pets or livestock, there will be no fee, but we, the rehabber, can't promise that. It's not something we have control over. Even when it's a vet you are familiar with and know they don't typically charge, I would still recommend saying "I've never known them to charge for euthanizing a wild animal before, but that would be between you and them," because you never know when their policy will change and you certainly don't want to end up paying the bill yourself! Rehabbers have enough expenses as it is.

(Note- one is more likely to receive help with an animal needing euthanasia if they show up with the patient vs. calling. Sometimes the front desk staff says no without ever approaching the vet with the situation. With a badly injured animal in tow, very few places will turn them away.)

Some vets tell the public they are not legally permitted to assist a wild animal, even if their state has no such law. I suspect it is easier and sounds less harsh than saying they don't want to. They may be uncomfortable dealing with species they are unfamiliar with. They may simply not have the time. Perhaps they don't want to start a precedent, fearing they will be asked repeatedly. They may not want wild animals brought into their hospital lest it cause an outbreak of disease. Even if unlikely, their clients could become distressed at having their beloved pet cared for in a facility where a wild animal is receiving treatment.

However, sometimes all it takes is for a rehabilitator to meet with the veterinarian, explain what she does, and establish a rapport for the vet to change his mind. He may be more likely to help if the rehabber: comes across as professional; is willing to assist (if needed) with a species the vet is not all that familiar with; is willing to be there at a scheduled time (not expect to drop in when convenient for them); and does not take advantage by bringing lots of animals to them for care. Only asking for assistance when truly needed rather than running every single patient by them will go a long way toward maintaining a positive working relationship with the veterinarian, not to mention it is not good for the wildlife to be exposed to all the people and domestic animals at a vet's office. (The exception, of course, is when the vet specifically works for your organization on site and it's expected he will check every animal.)

Note: see Transporting a sick, injured or orphaned fawn on pg. 63.

Adult deer hit by car

One question you should ask when called about an injured deer is whether it is an adult or fawn. Some people will think it's a fawn because they don't realize otherwise. Many tend to think adult deer are larger than they are. Therefore, ask them to think of a breed of dog this deer is comparable in size to and then have them estimate a weight based on that. That should at least get you in the ballpark.

(Personal anecdote:- although I often have people mistake adult deer for a fawn, one of the most shocking involved someone calling about a "newborn." They told me it couldn't be more than a few hours old. When I asked for a weight estimate, they said "it can't be over 100 pounds." Fortunately they could not see my face and thankfully I was able to maintain my composure. I gently explained a deer that size was not a baby. The rest of their questions were equally bizarre. For example, they were concerned that their dog who chased this "baby" might now have a taste for blood. Since they slept with the dog, they were nervous about their safety. I answered their questions professionally and thoroughly without even a hint of a snicker. I saved any giggles for when I recounted the conversation that evening to my husband. No doubt, you will have your own unusual calls about deer, as well. I believe it is important to always treat the public with sincerity and respect, though I admit it isn't always easy.)

Find out your state's regulations about a fawn rehabilitator handling adult deer. They can be extremely dangerous and should only be handled by persons who know what they are doing and have the correct equipment and sedatives.

If your state does not allow you to go out on injured adult deer calls, you may still be able to offer guidance via telephone. Here are some questions to ask.

Is the deer standing or lying down? If he is standing, what is he doing? Going in circles? Falling down and getting back up? Trembling? A deer that is standing on all fours but going in circles or not running away may be suffering head trauma. It is possible the deer will recover with time. If it can be safely accomplished, the deer should be guided out of the road into a pasture, wooded area, or relatively safe place and given time to recover.

A head injured deer should not be confined because if he "comes to," he is going to bang into everything in sight. He could further injure or kill himself, not to mention the damage he can do to the vehicle, home, or enclosure he is restrained in. It is okay to confine him in a barn stall or fenced-in area if the person lives on a large piece of property suitable for deer, and can stay with the deer continually. That way if the deer does recover and begins bouncing off the walls, the door or gate can be quickly opened and the deer set free immediately. Just be sure they don't stand between the door and the deer's freedom or they could find themselves mowed down!

If the deer is unable to stand, ask if he is making an effort and cannot get up, or is he not trying. If he is not striving to stand, the deer should be given some time to be sure he simply isn't "knocked senseless." If the deer is trying to stand and cannot, or if time goes by and he continues to lie there and not try, then the best advice is euthanasia. How euthanasia of injured wild animals is handled varies by state. You (or the caller) should contact the appropriate agency in your state. In some cases this would be a wildlife officer, in others a police officer or highway patrol officer may handle it.

Often the caller will swear the deer "just has a broken leg" and gets upset that you are recommending euthanasia. Assure them that any deer with a single broken leg would be long gone. A three legged deer can move faster than they might imagine. For him to be unable to stand (or remain standing) means serious, extensive injuries are involved...a cracked pelvis, multiple broken legs, broken back, i.e. injuries the deer cannot recover from. You can explain that even if a veterinarian could be found to do the extensive surgery, there are many months of recovery time and physical therapy to consider. An adult wild deer will likely kill or paralyze himself in captivity and cannot be kept tranquilized for months on end while recovery takes place. That is impractical for any species, but especially a ruminant who can die from complications when they go long periods without standing.

As long as you ask lots of questions, listen to what the caller has to say, show concern, and give reasonable explanations, they will typically come to terms with the euthanasia recommendation as long as they understand it isn't that you simply don't want to be bothered.

Some people ask if they can keep the carcass for meat once the deer has been euthanized. Again, each state has different regulations. Learn those rules in advance so you can properly advise the public when asked. However, if drugs of any sort were used, then the person should not take the body for meat.

States that allow a person to keep the deer for food may require a special permit. Most wildlife officers carry the paperwork and, in some instances, highway patrol officers do, as well. In many states, persons caught with a dead deer in their possession out of season or without a proper license or tag can find themselves in serious trouble even though they did not hunt the deer. Again, learn what the laws are in your state and be sure you correctly advise the public so no one is fined or jailed.

Most insurance companies require a police report if a car is damaged in an accident involving a deer. Advise the caller not to leave the scene until the proper authorities have assessed the damage and the correct paperwork has been filled out. (In cases where the deer needs to be euthanized, since officers must be called out to do the report anyway, often they can put the deer out of his misery while there.)   (See When a Deer Cannot Be Saved: Euthanasia Options on pg. 113)

Putting out food for deer

Deer rehabilitators are sometimes asked what foods to put out for deer.   Other times the fact the caller is putting out food comes up in conversation on another deer matter.   Either way, your input is important.

Putting out food for deer (or other wild animals) is controversial.   Some believe it should never be done.   Others feel we have taken so much from wildlife that putting food out is only fair.   Others fall somewhere in the middle, believing one should only put out food during severe weather.

Before discussing which foods are safe for deer, I think we should first look at the issue of whether to feed at all.

Viewpoint 1: Never put out food for deer

Those with this point of view believe that rather than helping hungry deer, feeding makes things worse.   If there are too many deer for an area to support, then one or more things will happen: all or most of the deer will become unhealthy because no one is getting enough to eat; the youngest, oldest and weakest will die of starvation; does may have only one, or perhaps no, young.

Providing food artificially will allow struggling does to survive and have the normal two babies, meaning there will then be even more deer trying to survive in an area that is already beyond capacity.   Much more artificial food must then be provided.   Does will continue to have more young and the young will grow up and produce babies, so the amount of supplemental feed needed will continue to grow exponentially.

Usually those who have this viewpoint of never feeding believe hunting, not putting out food, will solve the problem of "overpopulation."

Viewpoint 2: putting out food is a good idea

Generally those with this viewpoint feel humans have taken so much from the wildlife it is only right we help however we can and, for them, that means food and water.   They don't do it to prevent starvation or to allow more deer than the area can support (at least that is not their objective), they are simply trying to make up for all the habitat (and thus food supply) that has been destroyed as we build houses, shopping centers, and fast food restaurants.

Persons in this category typically also feed because they enjoy observing wildlife.   You often hear them boast of the large number of deer that come to their yard each evening to eat. They may joke about the expense it has become, but say the joy they get is worth the cost.

Viewpoint 3: feed only in bad weather

The people in this category do not believe in year-round feeding, but if the weather is particularly dry, wet, cold, or hot, or if there is an excessive amount of snow, they feel it is acceptable to put out food in those cases.   Except for extreme situations, however, they believe in letting wildlife find food as best they can.

Some issues to consider:

- For those that put out food for deer (or other wildlife), how do the neighbors feel about this?   Feuds sometimes develop over this very subject.

- Feeding deer/wildlife concentrates animals in a given area, making it more likely to spread disease and parasites.

- In very cold or snowy weather, deer will gather in a protected area and remain still to conserve energy.   The area is selected for its protection against wind, not whether it provides food.   Staying out of the wind is more critical than food, especially since the nutritional content of natural foods is going to be low in winter anyway.   If a deer eats available browse during extremely cold weather, he must create enough additional body heat to thaw the frozen twigs before they can be digested and utilized.   This can burn up more calories than is gained. Therefore, it may seem that putting out food is a positive thing.   However, one must consider how to get the food to the deer.   If deer are conserving energy in the wind-protected area and you carry food to them, you will likely startle them out of that space, causing them to burn calories.   Even if they return and consume the food provided, will it be enough to make up for what was used?   If, on the other hand, you place the food far enough away you don't spook them, they would have to leave their protected spot to find the food. So, it isn't as simple as it may seem.

Certainly planting trees, shrubs, and plants beneficial to wildlife is a more natural way of providing food. If they have acreage, they should learn the proper way to manage the land so it provides good habitat. Our land is 16 acres of nearly all trees and I always thought this was ideal for wild species. In fact, cutting down even a single tree seemed sacrilegious to us. However, in talking with a biologist, as well as researching the subject, I myself learned mature woodlands aren't nearly as wildlife friendly as I thought. So encourage the caller to talk to their local wildlife biologist or agricultural extension agent to learn what plants and habitat are best for the local wild animals.

For those that are going to put out food for deer regardless, advise them on what to feed and, as importantly, what not to feed. A large number of people put out deer corn. This is a poor choice for a number of reasons (see Feeding Instructions - foods to avoid on pg. 43). Deer should also never be fed bread or pastry. Since they are vegetarians, meat or anything that contains meat byproducts should never be put out for them. Apples are okay if offered in small quantity. Goat chow, the same as we feed fawns, is a much better choice than most of what people put out for deer.

"Nuisance" deer

You will sometimes be called by people who want to get rid of deer in their area. The biggest complaint is usually landscaping plants being devoured, sometimes the garden. Contact your area's wildlife biologists for advice on legal and humane methods to keep deer away, plants that deer generally find distasteful, and methods of discouraging deer. Ask if they prefer you have the person call them or do they mind you passing along this information to callers. Some biologists are fine with you sharing this information since they are often overworked and bombarded with calls. Others want to handle things themselves since it is part of their job and they want to be sure the correct information is given. Either way, they will appreciate being asked. It's a good idea to get to know the wildlife officials in your area. They can be an invaluable source of information and assistance.

Questions on deer hunting

Other calls you may receive from the public revolve around deer hunting. The folks you are most likely to hear from are those opposed to hunting, either in general or specifically on their property.   They want to know when deer hunting season is, what they can do to legally keep hunters off their property and so on.

This is a subject best handled by the agency overseeing hunting in your state.   Wildlife enforcement can advise when deer hunting is allowed, what the regulations are, what you must do to properly post your land, what to do if the laws are being broken, etc.

I advise getting an annual copy of the book they give to hunters.   This will help you keep up with changes in the law, when deer are "in season" and what they can legally be hunted with at certain times of year.   If you get in a deer shot with a gun during bow-hunting only season, you will know to contact authorities.   It doesn't matter if you are for or against hunting, it is still a good idea to know what the rules are, if for no other reason than to know when they are being broken.

As to whether deer hunting is a good or a bad thing will depend on who you ask.   One might assume if you are a rehabilitator you would be against hunting, but that is not always the case.   There are some rehabbers who are pro hunting, some are hunters themselves.

I have personal views on hunting, just as everyone does, but I rarely share them with the public.   When we formed our non-profit organization, we decided we would not take a public stand on certain topics, hunting being one.

Because I am a vegetarian, and have been for decades, I do not eat meat of any type, so it would probably seem logical I am not into hunting.   However, I am always surprised at the number of people who do eat meat, yet take offense at hunters killing deer for food.   They will say to me with a completely straight face and sincere heart - "I cannot understand how anyone could kill such a beautiful animal."   Or "Why would anyone kill a precious deer when you can go to the grocery store and buy meat?"

I want to tell them (and sometimes do, depending on how receptive the person appears) that while the meat counter may be piled with nice, neat styrofoam packages of countless types and cuts of meat, that does not mean the animals lived a nice, neat life.   Maybe they don't know about factory farms and the horrible conditions animals are kept in, the manner animals are transported to the slaughterhouse, and the slaughter process itself.   The deer killed for meat had the much better situation.   Until the kill shot, he had a wild and free existence.   He got to live a natural life.   He was not confined in a space so tiny, he could not turn around or scratch an itch.   He was not pumped full of drugs and hormones designed to do nothing except make him bigger and fatter so he could be slaughtered sooner for more profit.   He was not crammed into a transport vehicle and made to go without food or water for the time it took to get to the slaughterhouse.   He wasn't hung upside down and killed on an assembly line.   For the deer, unless he was wounded instead of killed, the death was quick and the animal did not know it was coming.

I am not saying I am for hunting deer.   I am saying if someone is going to eat meat from a supermarket, they are probably not in the best position to criticize those who hunt deer for food.

Hunters often find animals in need of rehabilitation, animals that likely would not have been found otherwise.   A number of patients brought to our facility are by hunters who seem to genuinely care about the animal.

I would much rather see woods than shopping centers, and lands protected for hunting, by default, help preserve the natural environment.

On the negative side of deer hunting, I believe it goes against the law of nature, survival of the fittest.   While I tend to root for the underdog, in nature it is the weak and sick that typically die so the stronger, healthier genes are passed on.   However, hunters are not shooting the weak and sickly, they are (most often) going after the biggest and healthiest, both for better tasting meat and better bragging rights.

I don't like the sound of guns disturbing the peace and quiet of the woods.   It makes me nervous.   I do not like being afraid to walk my own acreage lest a stray bullet finds me by mistake.   I also do not like people hunting with dogs, at least not where the dogs chase and tree an animal, then the hunter comes along and shoots it.   I do not understand the sport in that.

So I guess the bottom line is, even for me, the issue is not as cut and dry as I used to imagine. However, how I feel about hunting means nothing to anyone except me.   Each deer rehabber has to make up their own mind how they feel about it, as well as whether to get into the issue with callers.

Injured deer on caller's property

Deer rehabbers often receive calls about a deer in their yard or on their property that has an injury, typically a broken leg.   They usually want you to come and take the deer to your facility to fix the leg or put the deer in a petting zoo.   They do not understand the improbability of either, which is where the rehabber comes in.   It is important to explain why, rather than just saying you can't, so they understand the issues vs. thinking you just don't want to be bothered.

Before I explain anything, I ask questions, just as I would with any other wildlife call, so I can ascertain what's going on with this deer. I've also found people feel more "heard" if given the opportunity to describe the situation. We've all made calls only to be cut off before we could complete what we had to say, or else listened as the person on the other end gave those demeaning "uh-huh, uh-huh, uh-huh"s. You hang up frustrated and angry because you feel they didn't hear you, so how do they know for sure they can't help? So allow the caller to tell you about this deer. It may be the thousandth call you've had about a similar situation, but for the caller, this is likely the first and only time they've had it happen to them.

Some questions to ask are:

- is the leg broken or has it been severed/amputated? Try to get details about the injury, such as where the break is, if any bone is exposed, and so on.

- is the deer using the injured leg at all?

- does the caller see or hear flies around the injury? (they may have to use binoculars to see and even then it may be difficult to tell)

- how well is the deer getting around?

- how "fresh" does the injury appear to be?

After I have asked a number of questions, I ascertain if the injuries are life-threatening and, if they are, I have to give the difficult news that euthanasia (which most likely will mean shooting the deer) is the humane answer.

If the injury is not critical, I explain why surgery or a petting zoo is not feasible. We'll start with the latter because it is the simplest to explain. A wild deer would never be suitable for life in a petting zoo. He would go bonkers at the sight of people and never allow them anywhere near him, let alone pet him. He would be extremely dangerous to the public in a captive situation and, more than likely, seriously injure or kill himself trying to escape.

As to why surgery is not feasible, that one takes more detail. As the caller will likely tell you, the deer does not stay in their yard 24/7. They may see the deer daily or only every couple days. So first you would have to find a wildlife official willing to camp out until the deer did show up. Next, the deer would have to be shot with a tranquilizing dart which can leave a deep wound; it's not a pin prick. The second the deer hears the rifle or feels the dart, he is going to take off like a shot. The tranquilizing drug does not take effect immediately. It can take 10 minutes or so to knock the deer out and he can cover a tremendous amount of territory in that timeframe, injured leg notwithstanding.   If it is a wooded area, it is next to impossible to follow the deer to see where he goes down.   Without knowing where he drops, you may never find him.   If you can't, he's lying out there, completely vulnerable, and no way for the "wake up" shot to be administered.   If it is a residential area, the panicked and drugged deer could end up in traffic, falling in someone's swimming pool, crashing through the window of a building, any number of disasters.

But, let's pretend everything goes perfectly.   The deer shows up the first hour the wildlife officer is there, the shot hits the right spot the first time, the deer is tracked and located when he goes down, then what?   A veterinarian has to be found to do the surgery, then there's the recovery time (see "adult deer hit by car" on pg. 119 about how long recovery takes and how a ruminant will kill himself in captivity if not kept sedated, or how he can die from complications of being down for a lengthy period of time).

However, rather than just telling the caller these facts and then hanging up, I feel it is important to take it a step further.   If they told you the injury appears to be an old one, inform them deer get by perfectly well with three legs.   The fact the injury is not new shows this deer has managed to get by for some time that way.

(Personal anecdote: I get calls about three-legged deer a lot and most of the time when I finish my spiel, as explained above, the caller is at ease and hangs up satisfied with the information.   One gentleman, however, was not at all pleased with what I told him.   He accused me of not caring and hoped I would be happy when this poor deer died a horrible death since it was obvious she could never survive with three legs.   About six months later, I received a call from the same gentleman and I was prepared to be lit into again. However, he wanted to tell me the doe had shown up with two fawns in tow.   Therefore, not only was she able to survive, as I had predicted, but had apparently been doing well enough to mate, carry young to term, give birth, and properly care for the babies.   He actually apologized.   I was flabbergasted.   Not that the deer did so well but the fact he was man enough to admit it and apologize!

On another note, my husband and I rescue and adopt special needs dogs.   One of our "kids," has 2 3/4 legs.   Now granted she is not a wild animal and doesn't have to fend for herself, but up until arthritis set in, she could run so fast, we could not begin to catch her.   I can only imagine how fast she would have been if she had three legs!)

If the caller tells me the injury appears recent, I recommend they purchase Purina goat chow and put it out near the area they are seeing the injured deer.   I suggest they sprinkle the chow with an herb called horsetail, as well as vitamin C, to help with inflammation and healing.   The chow is sticky from the molasses so supplements will not blow away and deer like the taste of both.

I realize the injured deer may never be the one to eat this food, but I also know he might.   If he does, it will help his injury.   If, instead, other deer eat it (or in addition to him), the herb and vitamin won't hurt them.

Often people ask about using antibiotics instead, but dosage is critical and they must be given regularly for an extended period of time.   A small amount in a hit and miss fashion does more harm than good.   Also, there's the matter of the good bacteria being killed off as well (see Common Ailments - a word about antibiotics - pg. 57)   In addition, since there's no way to prevent other animals from getting into the food, we wouldn't want them getting the antibiotic.

Garlic is an excellent natural antibiotic, it does not destroy good bacteria, and there isn't the problem with dosage so it could be added to the chow as well.   However, whether the deer will eat goat chow with garlic is questionable.   Some animals like the taste and others do not, so I typically just recommend the horsetail and vitamin C.

Though I am hopeful the injured deer might actually get the food and herbal "meds," the other reason for suggesting this is the caller wants to feel they are doing something to help. It is difficult to be the person seeing the injured creature in their yard.   This gives them a way of potentially helping.   Last, but not least, I tell the caller to keep in touch and let me know if the situation changes, either for the better or worse.   I never want them to feel they cannot call back.   Some situations require more than one conversation to resolve and sometimes people just need to share their concerns with someone knowledgeable.

Deer in unsafe area

We often get calls from the public concerning deer (adults and/or fawns) in the middle of a highway or along an entrance ramp (or sometimes a busy section of town).   The bottom line is it's not a particularly safe place for the deer.   They are concerned he will be hit by a car, and want "something done."   The sad reality is this type situation is better left alone. Anything anyone (professional or not) attempts to do to help the deer is only going to send him running into traffic.   The deer got to where he is on his own.   He has a much better chance of getting out of the area safely himself than if someone tries to "help."   (See "Injured Deer on caller's property – above- for details on why sedating the deer is not feasible.)

LESSER KNOWN DANGERS TO DEER

Lightning

Deer, just like people, can be struck by lightning. They can be standing close to a tree or next to a wire fence and be hit. Rehabbers sometimes go out after a storm, find dead deer, and think the noise frightened them to death. If a deer has been hit, there should be burn marks on the body. Sadly, sometimes several deer are killed during a storm due to their tendency to huddle together.

Predators

Coyotes kill (or maim) deer, particularly fawns. Eastern coyotes are larger and weigh more than western coyotes, but both are easily able to kill a fawn.

There aren't a lot of cougars any more, but in areas where you do find them, they are very capable of killing deer.

Wolves are good at hunting deer, as well. However, there simply are not a lot of wolves around.

Bobcats can take down adult deer, but if they kill a deer at all, it's usually a fawn. However, deer (fawns or otherwise) are not high on a bobcat's list of prey. They prefer much smaller animals.

Deer fur is often seen in fox scat, but that is due to scavenging dead deer, not killing them. Foxes may manage to kill fawns if they are sick, weak or injured to begin with, but it is rare.

Trains and planes

We are all sadly aware of how often deer are hit by cars, but may not realize they are also hit and killed by trains and airplanes. In winter months where snow is an issue, deer will often walk along railroad tracks because they're clear. Deer caught off guard can panic and be hit. There is a photo making the rounds on the internet of a deer hit by a train, flung into the air, and landing on power lines. Can you imagine being the person at the electric company who took that call?

Rural airstrips often have tender plant material along the runway where it's continually mowed. This attracts deer and there have been instances of them being struck by planes.

Misc.

In addition to the above dangers deer face, they have been known to fall through ice on a frozen pond, get electrocuted by downed power lines, impale themselves on fences or branches, get stuck in the crook of trees, become bogged in mud and unable to get out, lock antlers with another buck and be unable to free themselves, fall into deserted wells, crash through windows, get trapped inside stores, attack faux yard deer and get their antlers caught, etc.   These are rare but you may, as a rehabber, have situations like these to deal with.   So in other words, be prepared for anything!

SOME DEER FACTS

It is my belief that to properly rehab a wild animal, you must know as much as possible about the species in their natural environment.   To know what is abnormal, you must know what is normal.   To best duplicate how a mother (or father) treats her young, you must know what that care consists of.   To understand why an animal does certain things, you must learn the reasons for the behavior.   To that end, this chapter and the next discusses basic white-tailed deer information and details about deer physiology.   This information will not only help you better care for fawns, but help you better answer the public's questions.

There are 17 genera of deer, 40 species and over 190 subspecies.   They can be found throughout most of the world, except Antarctica.   Deer were not native to Australia and New Zealand, but introduced.

In North America, deer include elk, moose, and caribou, as well as the exclusively American genus known as *Odocoileus*, which contains two species - whitetail and mule deer.   (There are subspecies of whitetail and mule deer, as well.)

Deer were abundant before the white man arrived, and were to eastern native Americans what bison were to the plains Indians.   They ate venison, made clothing from the hide, used sinew as thread, created tools from bones, used hooves to make glue, stuffed hair into moccasins for insulation, and fashioned weapons from antlers.   No part was wasted.

When the white man settled here, deer were extremely important to them as well.   Not only did they provide food and clothes, but were traded with Europe for cash and supplies.

As with many species, the white man over-hunted deer and, for a time, they were nearly extinct.   At the end of the 19th century, deer were so scarce that simply spotting tracks made local headlines.

Fortunately wildlife laws were enacted and, with time, deer began thriving again. This is especially true of the whitetail because they have the broadest range and can survive in the greatest variety of habitats.   They live in woodlands, swamplands, river bottoms, and forest edges.

Normal body temperature for a deer is 101 - 102 degrees F.

DEER PHYSIOLOGY

Fur

Deer go through two complete molts per year.   A winter and summer coat are very different in texture, color, and function.   In general terms, however, a white-tailed deer is tan with white circles around the eyes.   The belly, inside the ears, and beneath the tail are also white. There's a white band around the muzzle and chin, white throat patch, and white along the inside of each leg.   There are also areas of black on deer, as well.

A deer's winter coat is more grayish brown, the summer coat more tan.   The winter coat looks and feels rougher than the silky summer fur.   Winter hairs are brittle, hollow, and filled with air which acts as insulation.   Below that is a very fine undercoat, soft like cashmere.   No one knows for sure why, but all the hair on a deer points backward except for the chest (aka brisket) which points forward.

A deer's fur is subject to fading ("bleaching") in the sun.   In spring, when a deer is shedding the winter coat, they often have a ragged, unkempt appearance because it sloughs off in patches.

When a deer has his winter coat, any exertion before the weather turns cold causes problems. He will stand, mouth open wide, rapidly pumping in air at a fast rate in an attempt to cool down.   Even with a summer coat, deer are susceptible to heat, which is one reason they feed late evening, at night, and early morning.

Scent glands

Deer of both sexes have numerous scent glands, which play an important role in mating, marking territory, etc.   Sebaceous glands produce a lubricating substance that keeps the skin and hair from drying out.   Sudoriferous glands, on the other hand, produce pheromones.

There are various external glands on a deer: preorbital, interdigital, tarsal, metatarsal, and forehead.

preorbital glands

Preorbital glands (called lacrymal glands) are tear ducts in front of a deer's eyes, approximately 7/8" long.   The glands are almost void of fur and are typically dark blue to black in color.   There is often a residue toward the bottom of these slits.   The preorbital glands contain both sebaceous and sudoriferous glands.   Deer rub these glands on branches and other vegetation.   Although the odor is not as strong as other scent glands, they do emit a distinctive ammonia-like smell.

interdigital glands

Interdigital glands are located between the center toes on a deer's hoof.   If you were to spread the toes apart and push away the long hair, you would see the opening.   Look closer and you would see hairs inside the gland.   These serve as wicks for the waxy substance secreted from sudoriferous glands under the skin.   Every time a deer puts his foot down, some of the scent rubs onto the ground.   The odor is distinct and strong.   It allows deer to track each other and to identify individuals.

tarsal glands

Tarsal glands are considered the most important of the glands.   They are the large, tufted patches found on the inside of each hind leg.   In fact, to an inexperienced rehabber's eye, it appears to be a cut until you realize it's an exact match to the one on the other leg!   The tarsal gland is not a gland in the truest sense since there is no actual opening or duct. However, beneath the skin are both sebaceous and sudoriferous glands sending secretions to the surface.   Though the tarsal glands do have pheromones, their primary function is a depository for urine.   Deer of all ages do this, not just adults.   To accomplish, a deer has to stand in an odd "knock-kneed" position, rubbing the back legs together while urinating on them (see Urination & Defecation on pg. 47).   The more dominant the deer, the more he urinates on those glands.   Dogs identify each other by smelling back regions, deer smell each other's tarsal glands.   As deer age, the tarsal glands take on a dark brown coloration, a result of urine staining.

metatarsal glands

Metatarsal glands are found on the lower half of a deer's hind feet.   Like tarsals, metatarsals are not true glands.   They are about an inch long, counting the hair tuft.

forehead scent glands

These are located in front and behind a buck's antlers.   Both males and females have glands in the forehead area, though males have a lot more.   These glands increase both in size and the amount of scent secreted during rut.   This is true for both sexes.   The most dominant buck will often have a darkened area on his forehead due to the amount of scent he is excreting.

Digestive system

Deer are ruminants.   They have four chambers to their stomach - the rumen (which is the largest, at least eventually), reticulum, abomasum and omasum.   Only the abomasum is "functional" when a fawn is born.   At birth, the abomasum is the largest chamber, but eventually the rumen outsizes it by a large margin.   Fawns are born with some of the bacteria they need to digest food, but require browse to help the other chambers develop and properly function.   Each chamber has a crucial purpose.

A four-chambered stomach is important for survival.   It allows ruminants to eat large quantities of food in the shortest possible time, then chew and digest it later in a safer place. When deer are gathering food, they are at a great disadvantage.   Their sense of smell and sight are occupied locating food.   Their hearing is compromised due to the sound of their own eating (have you ever tried to listen to the television while munching potato chips and had to turn the volume up?)   Deer prefer to feed facing into the wind so the smells of predators/danger will waft toward them.   Deer do not feed in just one spot so as to avoid becoming a "sitting duck."   If you watch deer in the wild, you see them take a bite of food, take a few steps, then take another bite.

Deer vary their diet seasonally, which is important to keep in mind when rehabilitating.   In spring, deer feed on the first succulent grasses and leaves.   As the season progresses, deciduous leaves become the number one food choice.   Later in the summer, deer supplement their diet with mushrooms and berries.   Fall is when apples and acorns drop to the ground.   In places where acorns are readily available, deer will forsake just about everything else for the nutritious nuts.   Once depleted, deer return to eating grasses, leaves (including those that have fallen off the trees), and other browse.   When winter arrives, food choices become slender and deer must resort to eating the tips of branches.

Deer are primarily browsers, meaning they feed on the leaves, shoots, and tips of branches. When there is little choice, they will graze on grasses and similar types of vegetation, but browsing is primary and preferred.

Because deer lack upper front teeth, they use the rough pad at the front of the mouth to grab plants and tear, rather than bite, them off.   This creates a jagged edge on the leaf, making it easy to tell which are being eaten on by deer vs. rabbits. When forced to graze, they use their lips to manipulate greens into their mouth rather than using their tongue like cows do.

Deer chew food just a couple times before swallowing. The food enters the deer's first section of stomach (rumen) which can hold as much as 8 or 9 quarts of roughage. It acts both as a storage unit for unchewed food, as well as a fermentation vat. The rumen is lined with spaghetti-like papillae that vary in length.

Although deer can chew cud standing up, they prefer to find a hiding spot and lie down. A deer can rest, even doze, while chewing cud but the head must remain upright. This process is practically automatic, though if a deer becomes startled it all stops immediately.

To properly break down plants and convert them to something their body can metabolize requires billions and billions of microorganisms that live in the stomach. This is why antibiotics should never be used unless totally warranted and then always followed up with beneficial bacteria. (See "Common Ailments - a word about antibiotics" on pg. 57).

Cud is a vegetative material regurgitated from the rumen back into the mouth. It's about the size of a lemon. When a deer is chewing cud, the mouth moves in a sideward motion of the lower jaw. Cud is rechewed approximately 40 times before being swallowed again. The purpose is to break food into smaller pieces, making it easier for the microorganisms to further digest it.

Once the particles are refined, they bypass the rumen and float into the reticulum which can hold food about the size of a softball. The lining of the reticulum resembles a honeycomb. Although some digestion occurs here, the primary function is to filter foreign materials.

It takes about 14-18 hours for food to be eaten, made into cud, re-chewed, re-swallowed, then passed into the reticulum. From there it goes into the omasum where major digestion and absorption occurs. The lining of the omasum is made of forty flaps in varying heights.

The final chamber of the stomach is the abomasum and its lining is very smooth with about a dozen elongated folds. Food leaves the abomasum as a soup-like liquid. It passes into a deer's 65 feet of intestines where most of the nutrition is absorbed into the bloodstream.

Movement

Ancestors of today's deer had five toes on each foot which allowed them to easily travel in the forested areas prominent in those days. The climate later changed, giving way to more open spaces. To escape trouble, deer needed to sustain speed which meant sacrificing those toes.   The thumb and great toe evolved away.   Deer began walking in a more "raised-up" position.   The toenails got longer, hardened, and changed into today's cloven hooves.

Hooves are made of keratin, the same substance as our fingernails.   Keratin is actually a form of solidified hair!   On a deer's hooves, the outer edge is firmer than the center.   During cold weather, the center retracts slightly, giving a concave appearance.   Only the outer rim touches the ground.   This makes for good traction on rough surfaces, but when it comes to ice or an oily road, one slip and a deer is in grave trouble.   He is rarely able to get back up again, often dislocating hind legs or straining front ones.   (This is only on slick surfaces.   Deer have little trouble getting up otherwise.)   Hooves continue to grow throughout a deer's life.   Walking on rocky soil helps keep them worn down.

Whitetail deer walk, trot or gallop.   As they walk, the hind feet are placed in nearly the same spot just vacated by the front.   The tendency is to walk slowly, often feeding as they go along.   They rarely run without a reason.

A deer's top speed is around 35-40 miles per hour.   Deer sometimes stay perfectly still when faced with danger.   Other times they "high tail" it out of there.   And high tail is exactly what they do.   As soon as trouble is spotted, up goes that big, white tail as they rapidly run away.   Deer are good swimmers, and can swim rapidly and for long distances.

Watching a deer sit or stand is fascinating.   To sit, he first lowers himself to his front knees, then the back end drops to the ground.   To stand, he rocks his weight forward to his front knees, then rises from the knees.   If a deer is frightened, however, he rolls up so all four legs are under the body.   Using primarily the back legs, the deer then springs to his feet.

Antlers

People often use the term antler and horn interchangeably.   However, they are not the same.   Horns are found on sheep, goats, antelope, cattle and bison.   They are permanent, not shed.   They grow throughout the animal's life.   If they break off, they do not grow back.   Horns are fed by internal blood vessels and grow from the inside out.   Typically both males and females have horns.

Antlers are true bones minus the marrow.   They are found on deer, elk, caribou and moose.   Under normal conditions, they are shed annually and usually only males have them. (Female caribou do have antlers).   Antlers grow from a base known as the pedicel.   Without that base, antlers are unable to form and grow.   If a male is castrated prior to the pedicels developing, he will never produce antlers at any time during his life.

137

Whitetail males are born with two black spots on the head, indicating where antlers will grow when he is old enough.   At around 2-3 months of age, the pedicels begin to form hard knobs.   At around 5-6 months, the knobs cause the skin to stretch, making them relatively easy to see.   A deer at this stage of antler development is known as a button buck.   If the fawn was born in the spring, then antler growth stops or slows way down until the following spring.   Growth appears to be photoperiodistic, meaning tied in to regular cycles of light and dark.

Initially, antlers are covered in fine hairs known as velvet.   Velvet covered antlers feel very warm due to a rich supply of blood vessels.   The purpose of the vessels is to carry minerals to the antlers.   Antlers are one of the fastest growing tissues, often 1/4" per day!

During the time antlers are developing and in velvet, bucks keep very much to themselves. In mid summer, when the antlers have toughened up, males are less "shy."   Testosterone causes testicles to enlarge, as well as the antlers to harden.   The blood flow stops and deer are more than ready to scrape the velvet off.   It is typically removed in just 24 hours by rubbing against young, pliable trees (not mature ones as some imagine).   Though blood flow has all but ceased, some remains so it will be bloody as it's scraped away.   After the velvet is gone, antlers lose their stained appearance and begin to bleach white from the sun.

"Encounters" with saplings continue even after the velvet is removed.   It strengthens the neck muscles so bucks can better carry their rack of antlers.   A male's neck enlarges during rut to act as a shock absorber during the impact of fighting with other males.   Fortunately bucks do more posturing and threatening than actual battling.

The strongest bucks do the majority of breeding and, therefore, lose their antlers earliest. Losing antlers is not painful, though the fighting that precedes it can certainly be!   Once the antlers fall off, the pedicels are slightly bloody and take on a mild putrid smell.

With so many deer, you may wonder why people don't find antlers lying around in quantity. One reason is while they appear large and majestic when paraded atop a buck's head, on the ground they are easily hidden under leaf litter.   Antlers are also eaten by rodents, foxes, even deer themselves gnaw on the bones for the calcium and phosphorus.

Average life span

White-tailed deer can live 11 or 12 years, but few in the wild make it anywhere near that long.   In fact, few bucks make it to their prime of 4 1/2 years.   Even in areas where does can be hunted, bucks are still the most sought.   Some hunters simply cannot abide killing a female.   Bucks, not does, are usually considered trophies.   The larger the buck, the larger the rack, the larger the bragging rights.   That mindset over a long period of time is responsible for the imbalance of does to bucks.

Females live to be older in the wild than males.   Captive deer typically live much longer than wild ones, provided they receive proper care.   The oldest captive whitetail deer on record (to date) lived 21 years.

Reproduction

To learn about fawns, we have to start at the very beginning...rut season.   In late fall/early winter (depending on where in the United States you live), mating begins.   Males are ready before females, leading to much frustration and aggression.   Bucks take out some of their disappointment on saplings which serve as mock opponents.   The larger males make what are known as "scrapes."   These are circular patches of torn-up earth made by pawing with the front feet.   Typically bucks urinate, sometimes defecate, in the scrapes.   Since only the biggest, most dominant bucks (generally) dare make scrapes, they act as a type of advertisement, letting others know of their presence.   Bucks lower on the social scale might use a scrape if the dominant deer is not around, but the right to make his own has to be earned.

Dominant bucks waiting for females to come into estrus, along with lesser males who won't be granted an opportunity to mate, seek sexual release through masturbation.   Unlike some mammals, there is no bone in a deer's penis.   In the relaxed state, the penis is folded into an S-shaped curve (known as the sigmoid flexure).   When erect, the penis straightens.   To masturbate the male simply rubs it against his abdomen.

As with many animals, mounting for non-sexual purposes is a sign of dominance.   It can also be practice for when the deer comes of age and social standing to mate for real.

Prior to a doe coming into estrus, she will not permit an adult buck to approach if she can help it.   She urinates, which the buck then smells.   He will raise his head and curl his upper lip, known as flehmening.   With the lip curled back, the doe's scent lands on the lining of the organ at the top of his palate, called the Jacobson's organ.   This allows most mammals and reptiles to not only recognize scents, but interpret their meaning.   If the female is not ready, this will be relayed in her urine and the buck will leave to find one that is.

Bucks are very dangerous during rut.   Though they obtain some release through masturbation, until actual copulation occurs they are very aggressive.   Though rare in the wild, in captivity does are often killed by a denied male.

Note: As rehabilitators, I feel it is our responsibility and duty to educate the public about how dangerous "pet" deer are.   Although imprinted adult females are treacherous, a buck is, by far, the most formidable.   This is why imprinted deer should not be released into the wild; they could harm or kill an unsuspecting person or animal.   If the public contacts you with a deer they've imprinted and now the novelty has worn off, you need to understand what you are undertaking.   If the deer is still very young, it is possible, with enough time and exposure to other fawns, to undo the damage but with older fawns or adults it is unlikely. If the imprinting cannot be undone, you need to consider if euthanasia is the humane, safe, and responsible thing to do for all involved, including the deer.   I agree it is not right he should pay the price for the ignorance or stupidity of humans.   It breaks our hearts to euthanize a deer for circumstances he played no part in.   But it would also be unjust to force an imprinted deer to live in a world he does not understand and where he could cause serious harm.

It is rare for males to fight with other bucks in their social group.   This is because they are familiar with each other and know who the dominant members are.   When two unacquainted males meet, however, they go through a series of displays and bluffs, feeling each other out to determine whether this newcomer can outfight them.   If one buck does not turn away and a fight breaks out, they battle with their antlers and front feet.

When a female does come into estrus, it is signaled in her urine, as mentioned above.   Still, she will not stand for the buck his first couple attempts.   When she does assume the position, copulation occurs rapidly and forcefully, often knocking the female to her knees. If the doe is successfully mated (in other words, becomes pregnant), she will have no further interest in that buck or any other.   If she did not become pregnant, she will go back into estrus about four weeks later.   This will continue every month until she is impregnated.

Gestation is 187-212 days (males are generally carried longer than females).   In North Carolina, most fawns are born in May.   However, because of an imbalance with the number of does to bucks in many areas, numerous fawns are born in June or July (second or third estrus babies), sometimes even in the fall.   Because many, if not most, hunters prefer to kill bucks, it created an imbalance in the male to female ratio and there are now nursing mothers during hunting season.   This means if those does are hunted, they leave orphans behind. Knowing this, hunters may be even less inclined to hunt females.   How the ratio should be returned to a more natural 50/50 is often debated, but the fact remains, the balance is off in many states (certainly in North Carolina).

When the time to give birth arrives, females want to be alone. Last year's babies are taken aback by their mother's sudden aloofness. For almost a year, she has been their world and they hers. Now she avoids them, sometimes driving them away with her front feet. For a young buck, this separation is often permanent. Young does, however, typically rejoin their mother after a week or two.

About 10-14 days before giving birth, the doe's udder will swell and turn pink. This is easiest to observe from the rear. The doe searches for a private spot to have her young, hopefully one with some type of shelter, but no nesting area is created.

When giving birth, a doe typically lies on her side and goes through labor pains, like most mammals. How much pain and effort she must endure depends on the individual, as well as whether it is her first time giving birth. As she strains, the fawn begins to emerge feet first. The doe continues to push and the fawn comes out a little further. When the little one is almost out, the doe rests for a brief moment before completing the birthing of her first baby. She may or may not stand for that final push, depending on how tired she is. She examines her newborn, licking him vigorously. Typically he tries to stand within minutes, then he nurses while the doe is lying down.

Approximately 20 minutes later, the doe will stop tending to the first born and go into labor a second time. Most does give birth to two. A first time mother or one that's not very healthy may have just one. Occasionally she will produce three, but the norm is two. Twins or triplets are not necessarily identical. As with humans, if a single egg divides the babies are identical, but if two or three separate eggs are fertilized, the siblings are fraternal. In the case of identicals the babies are the same gender, so if one fawn is male and one female, you know they are fraternal. If they are both female or both male that does not necessarily indicate they are identical, however. All identical twins are the same gender, but not all same gender twins are identical. Fraternals are more common.

About 20 minutes after the final fawn is born, the mother eats the afterbirth. This is done both for nutrients and to keep away predators that might be attracted by the blood and tissue.

After all this, the doe is, understandably, exhausted so she will simply lie with her newborns curled beside her. As soon as she can, however, she moves them to a different area. Even though she gets rid of the afterbirth, fluids will have seeped into the ground that can attract predators.

Beyond the birthing

Average birth weight is 5 - 8 pounds (this can vary by region). When born, a fawn's legs are much longer proportionally than they will be as he grows. The muzzle is also shorter and seemingly out of proportion, as well. The jaws will lengthen as the fawn ages, making way for the permanent teeth.

Fawns are born with sleek, spotted coats. A doe does not stay with her young the first couple weeks of their lives. As a safety precaution, she places them in separate areas. That way if a predator finds one, it reduces the chance he'll find both. The spots (of which there are around 300), combined with the fawns remaining still, make them difficult to see.

The doe returns to nurse and groom her youngsters numerous times throughout the day and night (though primarily at night). The milk the mother produces the first few days is a thick, rich, yellow substance known as colostrum. It is extremely important to the fawn (as it is with all mammals) because of the antibodies it contains against disease and illness. (See Supplements on pg. 49)

Fawns pull on the nipple, then butt upward into the udder with considerable force. Fawns nurse for 5 - 10 minutes each feeding. They gain about 10% of their birth weight each day for the first week, then about 5% per week after that. Deer milk is around 12% butterfat compared to 5-6% for a cow. After three weeks, the butterfat content drops to around 8%. Oddly, as the fawns age and the amount of milk the doe produces decreases, the percentage of butterfat rises again. It reaches around 18% shortly before fawns are weaned at 5 months of age.

Fawns consume between 5 - 8 ounces per feeding the first week. As they get bigger, their intake increases. As discussed in the chapter on digestion (pg. 135), for the first two weeks, milk goes into the fawn's abomasum. Around 2-3 weeks of age, fawns begin eating greens (browse) and this allows the other chambers to develop, then function. Up until the fifth week, however, fawns cannot survive in the wild without their mother's milk because the rumen has not developed enough microorganisms for sufficient digestion of green material.

Newborns spend nearly all their time curled up in the location their mother tells them to wait. They get up to stretch their legs or move into a more comfortable spot (for example, if it gets too hot, they may move to the shade), but do not wander far from where mom left them. Fawns are curious and will lie with their heads up, checking out all that is going on around them. At the first sign of danger, however, their heads drop and they lie still and quiet, making themselves as small as they can. Ears are held back, but the eyes remain open.

Between week one and two, fawns make it difficult for the mother to leave after nursing. They are not yet old enough to follow her around, but want to! Sometimes she must repeatedly instruct them to lie down, often pushing with her head or foot. As with all youngsters, some are more obedient than others. (The public often runs into this, as well, when trying to put back a "kidnapped" fawn.)

When a doe returns to where she left her young, she softly calls to them. She recognizes her babies, not by sight, but smell. After the fawns are around two weeks old, they remain with mom, often grazing alongside her.

Communication

Deer communicate with each other in many ways. The method they choose depends on what they are trying to say and the circumstances.

An alarmed deer will sometimes stand in place and stamp a front foot, usually more than once. The tremors are felt by other deer in the area, alerting them to the concern.

Another signal involves a deer standing with his body tense, leaning forward. The head and neck are lowered and extended as the head bobs up and down. This behavior also lets other deer in the area know there's potential danger.

Of course, the best known alarm is the raised white tail as a deer runs off. The fanned-out tail alerts others to danger, as well as gives fawns an easy-to-see way of following their mother.

Another way deer notify each other of danger is through sound. With mouth closed, air is forced through the nose causing the nostrils to flutter and results in a loud snort. Deer make this sound when surprised or frightened. The noise alerts other deer of potential danger and they prepare to flee if necessary. A higher-pitched whistle-like vocalization is made with the mouth open instead of closed and indicates immediate and unmistakable danger, nothing "maybe" about it. When deer hear that sound, they explode into a group run. There is no hesitation, everyone flees.

Unless deer know for certain danger is immediate, they do not blindly run about. They understand that taking off in a mad tear without knowing what or where the threat is, they may unintentionally head right to it.

Deer vocalize for reasons other than peril. Does emit a soft sound to their fawns. Bucks utter a deep, loud grunt when trailing a doe coming into estrus. Fawns bleat, a sound similar to a calf or goat.   Fawns frightened or injured can belt out a horrific sound, similar to a scream.   It is extremely disconcerting for a rehabber trying to help.   Fortunately those screams are rare because, trust me, they give you cold chills and break your heart.

There are other, more subtle ways, deer communicate - some of them biologists are aware of and some they are just beginning to discover.   All animals, humans and non, have body language their species understands, but others may not.   The same is true of deer.   There are many stances deer take that speak volumes to other deer, but we have yet to ascertain their meaning.

DEER ANOMALIES

Piebald deer

Piebald deer have normal deer colors, just not in the right places!   They have excessive amounts of white fur.   Obviously white is normal around the eyes, inside the ears, on the belly, beneath the tail, around the muzzle and chin, throat patch, and inside each leg.   Piebalds, however, have white in areas that should be tan.   How much varies for each deer.   Some have a small amount while others have far more white than tan.

In addition to the unusual pattern of coloration, piebalds typically have one or more of the following deformities: short, malformed legs; curved/arching spines (scoliosis); bowed nasal bones; deviated leg joints; short mandibles; malformed internal organs.   They often do not grow to be as large as other deer.   Depending on the extent of these issues, they may not survive long term.   Some are unable to properly nurse, therefore die shortly after birth.   If they are badly deformed, they cannot keep up with the herd, and fall prey to predators.   If abnormalities are few, they can live like regular deer.   If they survive to adulthood and breed, they can give birth to normal deer, piebalds, or albinos...sometimes some of each.

Albino deer

A true albino is totally white with pinkish eyes, nose and hooves.   You can actually make out white spots on an albino fawn because they are a slightly lighter or brighter shade of white.

Albinos can live to adulthood, breed, and have young.   However, many die young due to health issues.   Albinos have problems seeing and hearing.   Their overall health is not good.   A mild illness that "normal" deer easily survive would likely kill an albino.   Albinos stand out and, therefore, make easier targets for predators, as well as hunters.   Some hunters, if given the choice between a regular deer or albino, would choose the latter because of the rarity, more of a "trophy" in their mind.   The same is true of piebalds and melanistic deer.   (Not all hunters feel this way, of course).   So for those that do live to adulthood, few live to be very old.   If they survive long enough to breed, they can give birth to normal fawns, piebalds, albinos, or some of each.

(Author's note: I have taken in several piebald and albino deer in the years I've been rehabbing.   They are not commonplace.   Few survived long term.   We had one young albino buck that had been hit by a car.   After surgery and recovery, he was released and we were so tickled.   However, he was again hit by a car and that time did not make it.

Because they have such trouble seeing and hearing, they have a difficult time avoiding situations that lead to injury or death.)

We often get calls from the public about an uninjured albino (or piebald). They want him captured and taken to a protected area, or want an ordinance passed to make shooting him illegal because he is "so special." We try to help them understand that being albino or piebald are not desirable traits to protect and pass on. That does not mean we advocate euthanizing them or providing them less security than a normal deer, but they should not be given more protection either.

Melanistic deer

A melanistic deer is dark brown due to an overabundance of pigment. They are a very pretty cocoa color. Like piebald and albino deer, they are relatively rare. Melanistic deer, however, do not seem to have the health issues piebalds and albinos do.

(Author's note: I have never taken in a melanistic fawn for rehab.   However, I am aware of melanistic deer not too far from my home. The females have given birth to both normal and melanistic fawns.   One gave birth to three babies - two with normal coloration and one melanistic.   In this very same area are albinos and piebald deer as well.   We have no idea why all three types are in that one place)

Antler anomalies

Though antlers are normal on female caribou, they aren't on white-tailed deer females. Antlered does fall into three categories. The first are true females. They can breed and nurse. They have normal female hormones, just not enough to suppress antler growth. The antlers remain in velvet.

The second are not true does. They have both a penis and vagina. The scrotum and testicles are inside the body. In spite of the female sex organs, the hormones are such that antlers form. This type never bears young.

The third are female deer with a tumor that produces male hormones. The doe may have both male and female reproductive organs. The antlers typically remain in velvet.

Now, to males. Just because the deer is a buck doesn't mean he will have normal antlers. Generally, antlers are symmetrical. Unusual shapes can be the result of injury, heredity, or mutations.   Damage to antlers happens more with white-tailed deer than mule deer, while mule deer antlers tend to suffer more genetic deformities.

As antlers are growing, they are soft enough to be bent.   As a result, deer may have an antler pointing one direction and the other an entirely different way.   Though unusual, deer have been seen with antlers pointing forward toward the nose, or sideways forming a football helmet appearance.

Another odd antler formation resembles a bed of coral.   The pictures I have seen look, to me, like the deer has a head of curls.   It's pretty bizarre, that's for certain.

An antler with a knot and hole in it is the result of a warble fly laying an egg while the antler is still soft.

Interestingly, if a buck is injured on his right side, especially the hindquarter area, his left antler will grow abnormally or show damage, vice versa if injured on his left.   Some theorize the deer, in licking his injury, tends to bang the opposite antler on trees.   Others believe that since the left side of the brain controls the right side of the body (and vice versa), injury to one side will show up on the opposite.

PHOTO SECTION

I wish the photos could be in color, but it is just too cost-prohibitive. Fortunately you can still see many details in black and white.

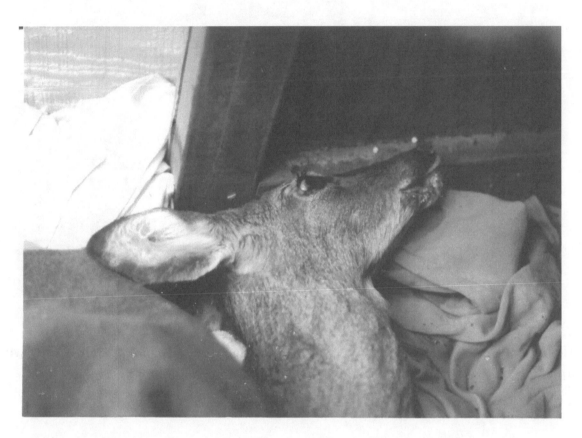

This doe ("Ember") was my very first deer patient. She had been hit by a car and paralyzed. If she had not died on her own, she would have required euthanasia.

(Author's note: At Kindred Spirits, all our patients get names. However, I did not list each of their names in the following photos. I know some rehab centers take issue with naming the patients giving them numbers instead. My personal opinion is, who cares? It's not as though the animals are going to be able to distinguish between a name and a number. You'll release them and they'll be forever scarred because they had a name? It's often the same facilities who get so worked up over things like this that allow a flow of volunteers working with each patient. I personally feel that is far more harmful than naming the animals. So if you want to name your patients, I see no problem with it, as long as you keep the caregiver to one and treat the animal as close to natural as possible.)

This little fawn was confiscated from someone who had her illegally.   Apparently they were mistreating her.   Note her torn-up face.   Her behavior indicated abuse as well.

This little buck ("Faison") was hit by a car, resulting in a badly injured leg and back.   Here he rests on a bed of thick foam to prevent bedsores.   He has a poultice on his leg.   Deer rarely recover from a back injury, and this fella was no exception.

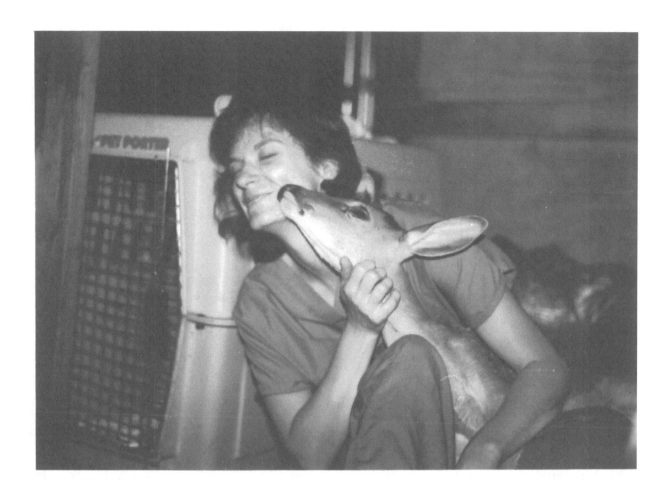

It takes time to win a wild animal's trust.   Here this paralyzed deer shows her appreciation. This is why it is important to have only one caregiver.

As mentioned on pg. 27 under caging information, two fawns can be kept together in one crate during quarantine if they are very small. These two fawns were delivered together in one crate, but this carrier is obviously too small for one of the fawns, let alone both. Fawns temporarily in a crate should be able to stand, walk around, and have plenty of room to sleep, use the bathroom, etc.

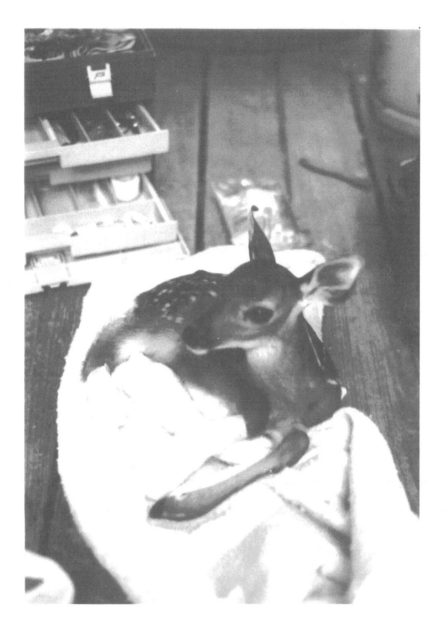

This is the fawn I referenced on pg. 66.   She was run over by a hay baling machine, severing three of her legs.   I cleaned and bandaged her limbs.   If there was any way I could have made all four legs the same length and let her survive as a short deer, I would have because she was so precious.   The sad reality, however, was she had to be euthanized.

A fawn in rehab.

As I talked about on pg. 84, removing maggots is a back breaking, time consuming task. Whenever possible, I do it outdoors on a sheet I can just pitch in the trash.　Of course it varies with each case, but as a general rule, it takes around three hours to remove an infestation of maggots.　By the time I'm finished, it's hard to straighten my back, let alone walk.

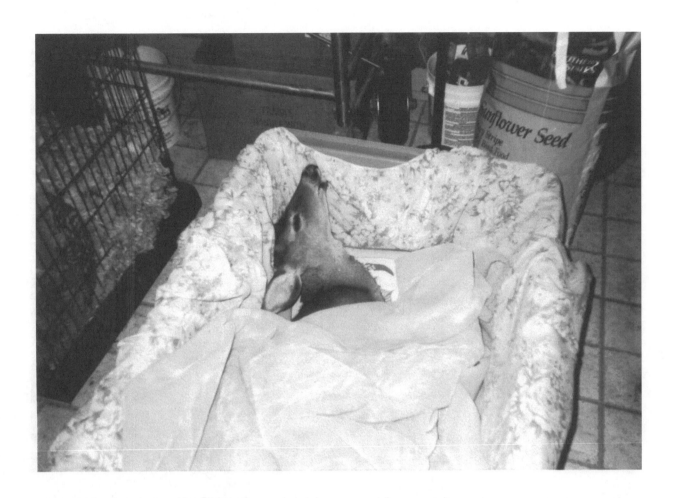

Here is another severely injured deer.   This one is suffering from a neck compression.   It often occurs when a deer rams himself headfirst into a solid fence.   If he doesn't break his neck, he usually ends up with a serious neck compression.   Although it is possible to recover from this major injury, it requires a ton of work and many, many months of physical therapy.   It is a slow, tedious process and more often than not, the deer dies from complications of being down.   Every rehabber I've guided through this has told me the same thing - they don't resent the time and effort they devoted to their deer, but would never do it again.   After having worked with several, I'd have to agree.   I think euthanasia is probably the best decision for all involved, including the deer.

This is a piebald.   As mentioned on pg. 145, a piebald is the normal tan, black, and white. However, the white in the wrong places.   Piebalds also tend to be short in stature, have curled under legs (note the front legs on this one), and a malformed jaw (note his short snout area).

The damage dogs can do to fawns is horrific. Here the top half of this fawn has been degloved. As severe as this injury is, it is actually mild compared to most dog injuries.

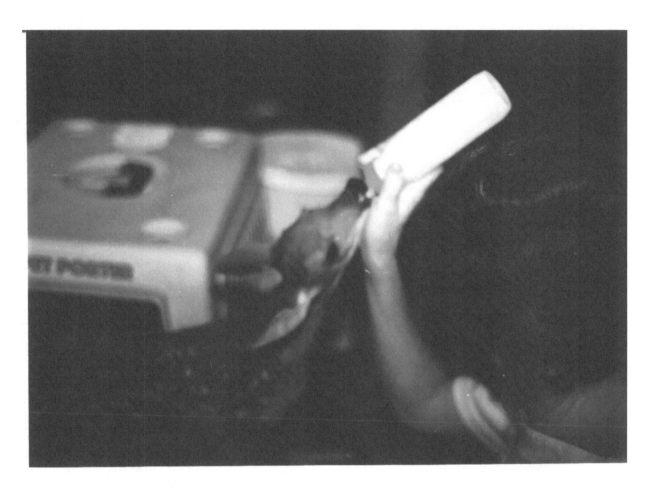

Note how I am using the palm on my hand to tilt the fawn's head slightly upward.   This is the proper stance for a fawn taking a bottle.

A deer suffering a neck compression rests on an air mattress to help avoid bedsores.   It is very bad for a ruminant to be down for long periods of time.

No, that isn't an over-exposed picture.   You are seeing an albino buck.   Albinos have problem seeing and hearing and are, therefore, often hit by cars, as was "Spark." One of Spark's antlers had to be surgically removed because it was broken off at the pedicel.   The other antler, as you can just barely make out, was turned upside down.

Although Spark did recover from his injuries and later released, he was hit by a car again and that time did not survive.

A little fawn being rehabilitated for release into the wild.

© 2016 by Dana Sims - all rights reserved

Another fawn being rehabbed.   It's amazing how each fawn looks different.

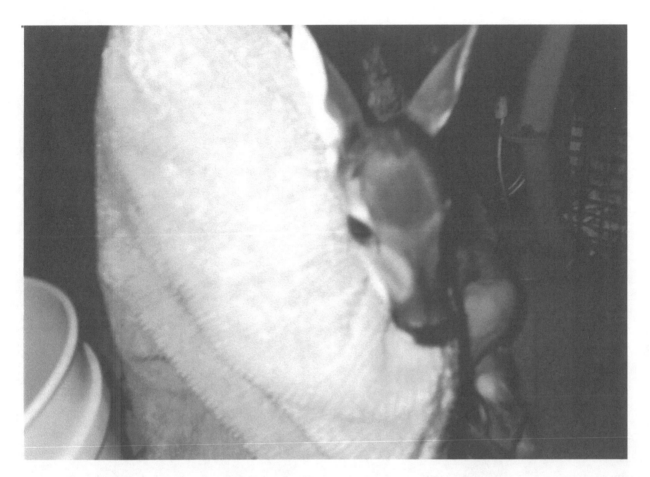

As discussed on pg. 64, it is important to properly hold a fawn. Note how close the little one is being held to my body. I am holding him firmly. It doesn't show in this picture, but the back legs are held by my other hand and are slightly outstretched to cut down on the amount of thrashing he can do.

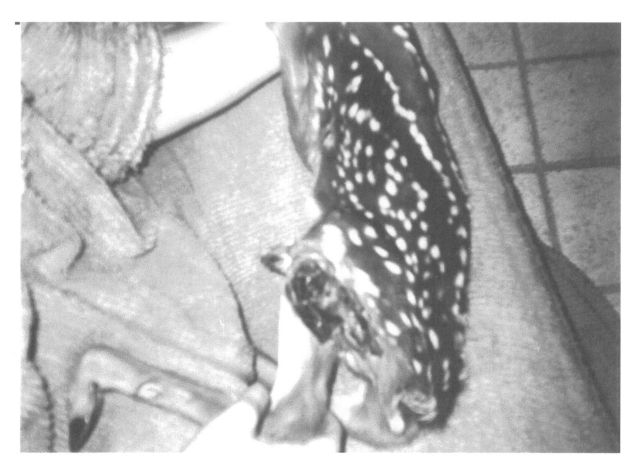

This fawn was badly injured by a hay baler. (See pg. 66 for further information on mowing injuries). The wound was very deep and affected the muscles and tendons.

A very sick albino fawn.

As mentioned on pg. 43, fawns are notorious for nibbling on your legs (or whatever they can reach). They can be quite aggressive and it hurts! Here a little fawn tries to nibble on my leg. Ouch.

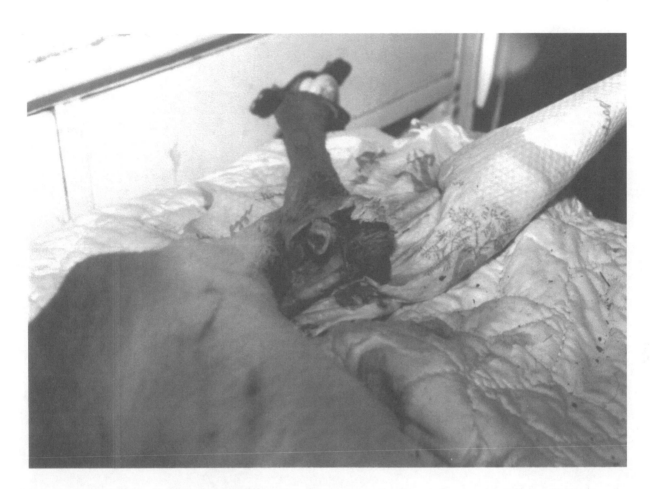

This deer was hit by a car.   One leg, as you can see, was snapped completely in two.
Believe it or not, if that was the deer's only injury, she would have been able to run off.
Given the fact the bone was exposed and the wound gaping like it was, the chance of
infection setting in would have been high had she managed to get away.   However, she had
a lot more wrong and she did not survive.

Another deer hit by a car.   Another severely damaged leg.   As previously mentioned, if one leg was the only injury, the deer would have run off and never been taken into captivity for treatment.

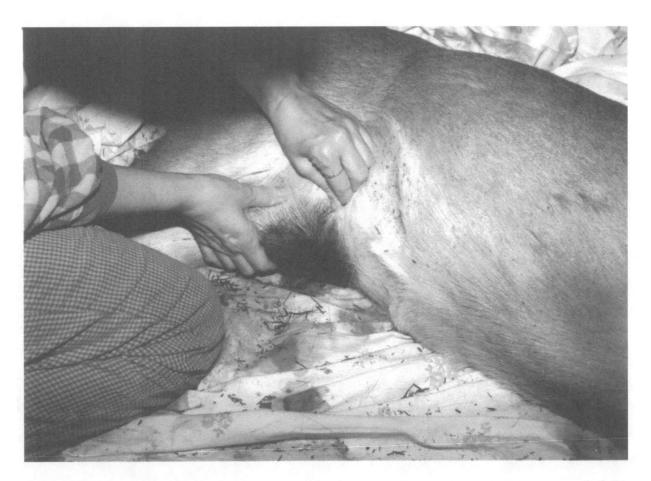

As you can see from the dark area, this doe was bleeding internally.   This was an adult deer and severely injured.   She did not survive.

© 2016 by Dana Sims - all rights reserved

This is not a normal position for a deer to lie in.

This fawn is alert and sitting in a normal sternal position.

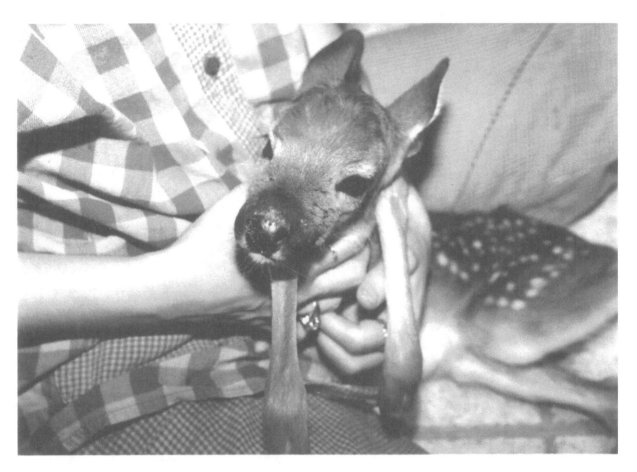

It took me a little while to figure out why the snout area on this fawn was so swollen. Turns out it was filled with maggots that had entered from inside his mouth/lip area.

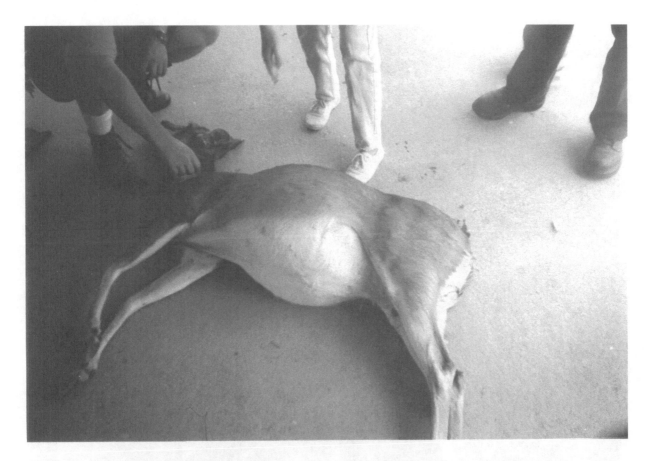

This doe had been hit by a car and paralyzed.   Dogs got to her and began tearing at her hindquarters.   Someone driving by saw this helpless doe being eaten alive.   They stopped and called me for help.   They said she was pregnant but I wasn't sure she hadn't simply bloated from being down.   Sure enough, she was definitely pregnant and near term.

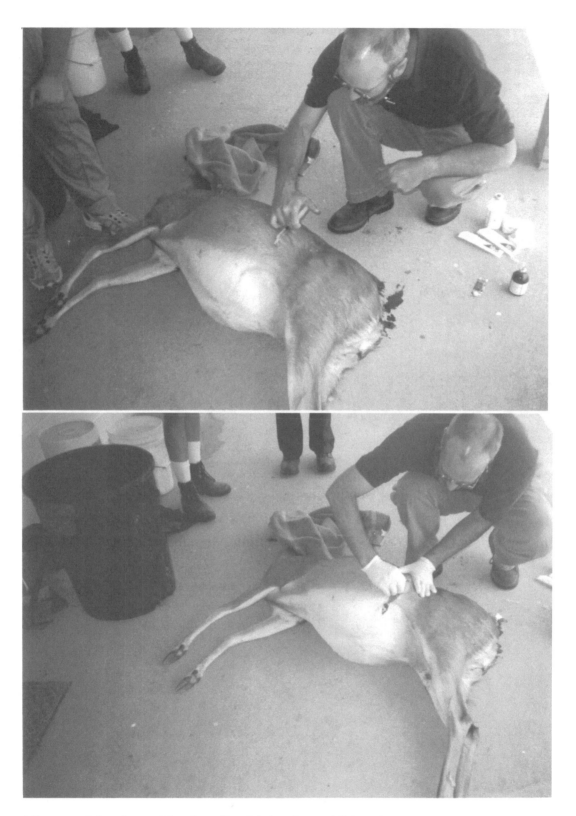

After numbing her with a localized injection of lidocaine, a veterinarian begins to perform a C-section. We could not put the doe completely under anesthesia because of the fawns.

There were three, yes three, fawns removed from this mortally wounded doe.   Sadly none of the fawns were breathing.   We worked hard, massaging, injecting stimulants, etc. but could only revive one.   I named him Tri, not only because he was one of three, but we tried so hard to save him.

Here Tri is getting oxygen as he struggles to beat the odds.

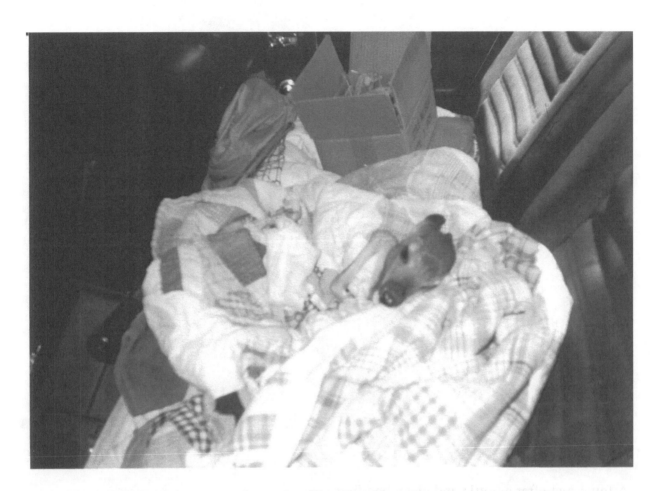

After keeping Tri on oxygen at the vet's office for close to an hour, he is finally strong enough for the trip to my facility.   I started him right away on colostrum.   Believe it or not, Tri survived to release.

A fawn just after a bottle and clean bedding.

Sometimes, no, many times, when rehabbing we have to make difficult decisions. When a fawn goes crazy and begins bouncing off the walls, especially when he's in a pen with others, if he doesn't calm down, you have to decide whether releasing him is better than letting him hurt (possibly kill) himself and the others. This deer would not calm down. He was going to break his neck, so I decided to release him. Although still nursing, he was technically old enough to survive. Still, it would have been preferable to hold on to him if possible.

This handsome fawn dons his winter coat.   Note how different it looks than a summer one. It's not sleek like a summer coat.

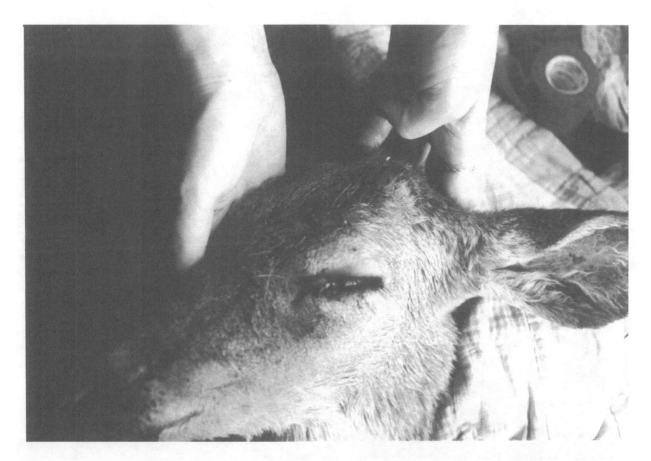

This poor deer was one of two someone shot just for the "fun" of it.   One died.   This one had been shot in his head.   Here he is after I sewed him up.   (I knew those home-ec classes would come in handy!)

A bevy of babies.   Aren't they beautiful?

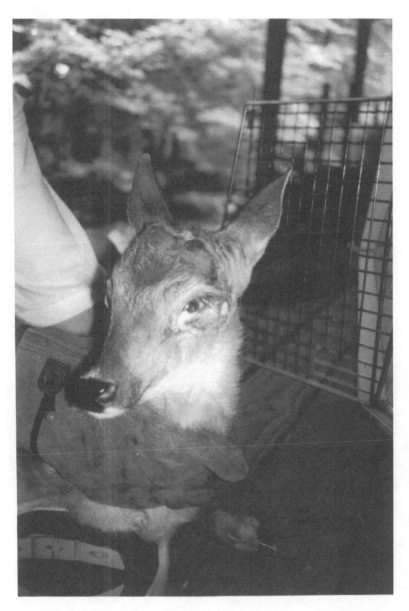

This poor little buck had a serious infection that affected not only his eye, but his brain.

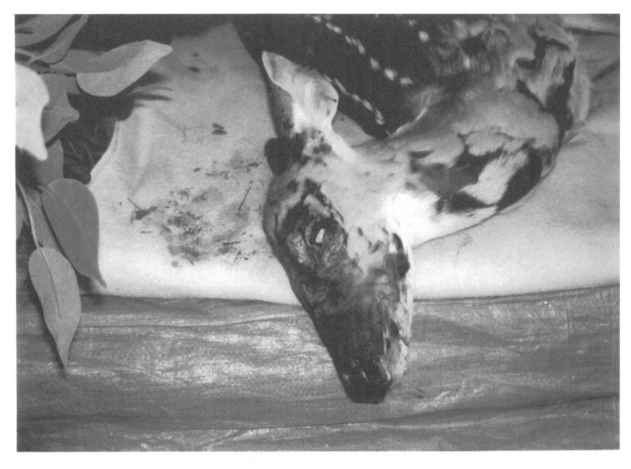

This poor young deer was hit by a car, ran into a cow pasture, and was then trampled by cows.   When I say on pg. 130 to be prepared for anything, this is a perfect example.

This fawn is shown in a transport box designed for a single fawn.   The state also had a trailer they used for transporting larger numbers of deer.   This was back when fawns were hard released.   For information on hard vs. soft release, go to pg. 53

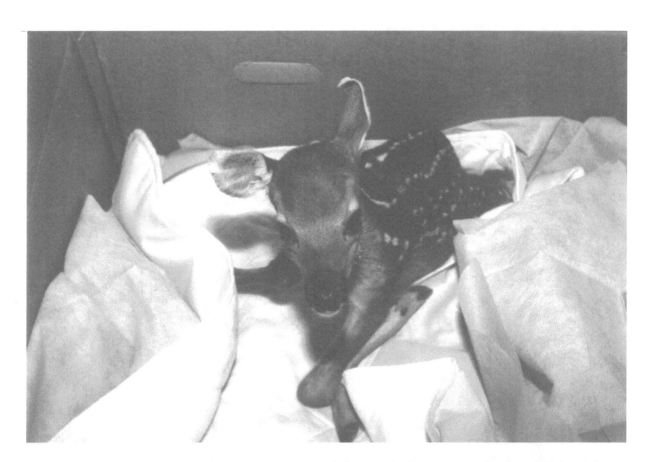

Note the curled ears on this fawn.   I once read that curled ears on a deer means health problems and that once the problems are cleared up, the ears straighten.   However, I have not found that to be the case.

This is an example of a feeding rack.   One picture shows the opening empty and the other with a bottle inside.   This particular one is made from wood and used on a chainlink fence.   Inner tubes cut to size are what is holding the bottles in place.   (They stretch enough for you to get the bottle in at an angle, but taut enough to keep it in the opening.)   This kind of rack allows you to place the bottles inside without going into the pen.   This particular rack holds 8 bottles so you are only seeing one small section.

No, this isn't a fuzzy piebald fawn. This is our precious Barney who left us for the angels at the ripe age of 18 or 19. I did not have fawns at the time the pictures were needed. I decided to use him to demonstrate the proper feeding position for a fawn you are bottle training. You will notice how I am holding his snout and the bottle, as well as tilting his head. As mentioned in the book, if you have a family dog that is easy going like Barney, then you can practice the proper method before you actually have to try it with a fawn. Obviously Barney is not struggling like a fawn would, but it will still help you get a feel for things before faced with the real deal.

ABOUT THE AUTHOR

Everyone assumes if you are a rehabilitator, you brought home every kitten, puppy, and baby bird when you were a kid.   Believe it or not, as a child I was scared of animals.   If someone had told me I would be working not only with animals, but bloody, maggot-infested ones, I'd have blacked out from lack of oxygen due to hysterical laughing. My college degree is in business administration with a minor in journalism.   So how in the world did I end up rehabbing wildlife?   Our love for dogs became well known locally and one day someone brought an injured bird instead.   It rather mushroomed from there.   State and federally licensed, we now take in everything from baby mice to black bear cubs...and nearly everything in between.

I have been a writer as long as I can remember, starting with poems for my mother once I learned the alphabet.   I recall a stanza from an early Mother's Day card - "She feeds us and clothes us and gives us a bath, but when she is mad she could cut us in half."   Hopefully I've improved a little since then!   For a time, I had my own magazine column which was neat.   As nature consultant for our local recreation and parks department, one responsibility (since 1989) is writing a quarterly newsletter called "Nature News."

My husband and I are avid environmentalists, as well as animal lovers.   Our furry children are all rescues with special needs (medical, emotional or both).   We currently have nine "kids."   We live in a small, rustic, hand-hewn log cabin on 16 wooded acres, the perfect setting for a wildlife facility.

I love plants/gardening, antiques, crafting, reading, time with my parents, crossword puzzles, nature.   Unfortunately, serious health problems have <u>severely</u> reduced my activities and mobility.   I want to get well so I can go back to helping more animals and people.   Still, I appreciate every day, I truly do.   I have a roof over my head, heat in the winter, food, an incredible husband, great parents, plenty of dog kisses...much to be grateful for.

ABOUT THE VETERINARIAN

<u>Charles W. Miller, D.V.M.</u>

Dr. Miller graduated from the North Carolina State College of Veterinary Medicine in 1992. He is a practicing veterinarian and owner of Triangle Veterinary Hospital in Durham, NC. Since graduation, Dr. Miller has been active in the treatment and rehabilitation of many wildlife species including the white tailed deer.

(Personal anecdote: Dr. Miller is as modest as he is brilliant and caring.   When I asked him to write about himself and his qualifications, the above is what I received.   The truth of the matter is Dr. Miller's resume is quite extensive and impressive.   He worked in the medical profession (humans) before becoming a veterinarian.   He is extremely intelligent and never ceases to amaze me with what he knows.   You ask him a question and he always knows the answer.

I first met Dr. Miller when I had a black bear cub with a serious, life-threatening condition. We could not find anyone in our immediate area willing or able to help.   We were so impressed with Dr. Miller, we began making the two hour (round trip) drive for him to be personal vet for our many furry children.   One such "child" was our 18 year old rescue, Barney.   Barney was at the end of his journey with us and, like most old dogs, he was no longer cute and cuddly (except to us, of course).   He was old, off-balance, incontinent, and his eyes were goopy and teary.   His formerly snow white fur had taken on a dark coloration.   He looked like a dog nearing death.   While I might anticipate someone petting his head or talking sweetly to him, I would never expect anyone, except us, to kiss and hug all over him.   Yet Dr. Miller did exactly that, eye goo and all.   We knew then we were in the presence of an animal lover and earth angel.

In spite of the fact Dr. Miller is always pulled in a hundred directions at once with his job, personal life, charity work, etc. whenever he's helping you, you never feel rushed.   He always makes you feel you are the most important issue at that moment.

The animals are lucky to have Dr. Miller and we are fortunate he was kind enough to share his medical expertise on deer with us.   His input makes this book complete.)

PERSONAL NOTES

PERSONAL NOTES

PERSONAL NOTES

PERSONAL NOTES

Made in United States
Troutdale, OR
09/29/2024